CW01507270

Preface

I was first introduced to Jeff Einstein about four years ago through his weblog on media and addiction, *Einstein's Corner*. I was immediately hooked on his viewpoint, and found it so intriguing that I sent him an email telling him that his insight was fresh and brilliant.

Jeff emailed me back and expressed his gratitude, and I'm happy to say that our first email exchange has since evolved into a special friendship. I think it's fair to say that we hit it off right away...

So when he told me that he was writing a book titled *Put God First*, I was instantly fascinated, and he indulged me by sending the first draft as soon as it was ready. In my opinion, *Put God First* nails THE PROBLEM of the 21st century: We have taken a flight from faith and are wandering in the proverbial spiritual desert as we feed our media addiction.

In recent years we seem to have moved well beyond the couch potato syndrome that defined our relationship with television and mass media through the mid-1990s. Our media choices have increased exponentially in the past decade, and today we might be better characterized as benumbed, spiritless spuds. Burt Lancaster, in the 1960 award-winning film *Elmer Gantry,* warned against the compartmentalization of spirituality when he said, "You can't go to mass on Sunday and cheat in business on Monday."

In today's media-saturated environment, what Jeff refers to as the *Great Age of Mediation,* we consign God and spirituality to ever-smaller and smaller compartments. Most of us no longer give the Lord a single day a week, or even a few minutes a day. Our faith continues to shrink as our media addiction continues to grow. And as our faith decreases, our fears increase.

Fear is the soul-destroying weapon that the media wield to cleave God from our lives. Thus, watching the news is no longer about information that we can use. It has instead become a high-speed conduit for instilling and fostering fear. Terrorism, bird flu, economic collapse, global warming, illegal immigration, killer storms; the list goes on and on. The main message, however, is always the same: *Be afraid. Be very very afraid.* Fortunately, however, the same media that advise us to fear everything also offer up a ready antidote with each and every warning: more media. "Stay tuned," they tell us.

In the *Great Age of Mediation* fear has replaced faith. So what can we do? Jeff's call to *Put God First* echoes the gentle and remarkable response of Ann Frank, a little girl whose generous spirit and great heart belied the sheer terror that held her and her world hostage in a terrible time:

> *"The best remedy for those who are afraid, lone-*
> *ly or unhappy is to go outside, somewhere where*
> *they can be quiet, alone with the heavens, nature*

Put God First

A Pocket Guide to
Quality of Life
in the
Great Age of Mediation

Jeff Einstein

I thank God and His greatest gift to me,
my little girl Cayla,
for their constant inspiration…

and God. Because only then does one feel that all is as it should be and that God wishes to see people happy, amidst the simple beauty of nature."

Unlike the fear and tyranny suffered by Ann Frank and millions of others during World War II, however, many of the fears and tyrannies that confront us today are self-induced and manufactured. Thus, in the titanic struggle with our own excess there are few easy villains in the traditional sense, in large part because – as Jeff suggests – we are very much complicit in our own addictions. For instance, while today's media landscape features legitimate global media cartels that function at times not unlike the illegitimate drug cartels of Colombia, it also – with the sudden and relentless onslaught of consumer-generated content – features millions upon millions of small neighborhood dealers, each with their own designer drugs to produce and sell.

Regardless of who produces and supplies the narcotic, however, the demand will continue to increase in proportion to the *promise* of a functionally limitless supply guaranteed by functionally limitless bandwidth. And as the supply and demand for more media escalate, so too do the dangers: Inertia and apathy, two of addiction's primary byproducts, flourish in the *Great Age of Mediation.*

Inertia is what makes addiction so difficult to bust, and apathy is what besets us when we repeatedly encounter the depths of our own inertia. Apathy then breeds apathy. As we multitask across a typical universe of HDTVs, laptops, wireless phones, PDAs and MP3 players, we think little and care even less about the people and things that aren't on the screens directly in front of us. We simply haven't the time to consider whatever isn't on the screen in front of us right now. So we visit less with friends and family, we volunteer less, we pray less and we sleep less, all so we can spend more time consuming media. In the end we find ourselves *connected* to people all over the world but *disconnected* from the people living in the same house and town. And the most notable estrangement, of course, is from God Almighty Himself.

As the amounts of time and money that we devote to our media addiction grow, time and money for all other relationships is compromised. Not only is our relationship with God short-changed in the process, but all of the other important relationships we need for healthy lifestyles and souls are imperiled as well: Our relationships with our children, our spouses, our friends, and our businesses are all offered up on the altar of our addiction to the media. How often have you heard or uttered the words, "I'm sorry, but I've been so busy..." in the past month alone? Of course we're all busy; we always have been, always are, and always will be. But nowadays we seem to have even less time than ever for the important relationships in our lives, especially our relationship with God. We find ourselves falling farther and farther behind in our lives simply because we spend so much of our precious time feeding our addiction to media each and every day. We are compelled to feed the beast, and we find that the beast – like all addictions – is insatiable.

Put God First is an *important* book. It shows us how to reintroduce God into our lives as a critical force for *moderation* in the *Great Age of Mediation.* It shows us how a return to *faith* translates into a return to *reason.* Although each chapter begins with a brief prayer, *Put God First* is by no means a preachy evangelical treatise. Nor is it a convenient and self-serving exercise in media bashing. No matter what your religion or your relationship to media, you'll find something of value – something immediately applicable to *your* life – in these pages. Jeff has written a book that speaks with wisdom and compassion to the 21st-century malady of maladies. Hopefully, by shining a light on the problem we will then be better equipped to develop solutions. Time, however, is of the essence. *Put God First* shows us how and where to get started...

Jaffer Ali
CEO of NextEra Media

Introduction

> *Dear God,*
>
> *Thank you for walking with me today. Thank you for the many blessings you bring into my life. Thank you for exposing me to new ideas, and thank you for blessing me with the freedom to receive or reject them. Thank you for the gift of free will. Please teach me to pray, and forgive my many weak moments. Open my heart and mind. Help me put you first in my life. Prepare me always to receive your word and do your will. Amen.*

Bless you, dear reader, and welcome to *Put God First*, a smallish book of big ideas conceived in response to an even bigger concern, namely:

> *We now seem to be passing through a most extraordinary and dangerous time in our nation's history. It's a time when profligate consumption – more media, more food, more sex, more money, more credit, more debt, more licit and illicit drugs of all kinds, more of just about everything except time – all but destroys any sense of propriety and proportion, estranges us from God, and threatens the quality of our lives and communities at every level of society, irrespective of race, gender, or social status.*

It's a time I call the *Great Age of Mediation*, and I believe that the simple but controversial ideas in this little book represent our best hope to survive our individual and collective journeys through it.

Put God First is all about the choices we make en route. It's about how we react as individuals and as a society to the culture of mass consumption that we invite into our lives in the *Great Age of Mediation*, and about God's role – or lack thereof – in the mix. It's about the wholesale Faustian exchange of time for endless false promises, and how that exchange threatens the quality of our lives on all levels – spiritual, physical, emotional, and social. It's about how the *quality* of our lives will improve dramatically when we learn how to put Him first. It's about invoking God as the primary voice of *reason* and *moderation* in the *Great Age of Media-*

tion. It's about how to do exactly what He instructs us to do in the very first of His Ten Commandments: put Him first. And it's about how everything else quite naturally follows…

In taking you from here to there, *Put God First* adopts a simple thesis, antithesis, synthesis structure as represented by three major sections: *The Quality of Life Defined, The Quality of Life Threatened,* and *The Quality of Life Redeemed.* Each chapter herein begins appropriately with a brief prayer to welcome God, thank Him, and always put Him first, and each concludes with a summary of bulleted chapter highlights for quick and easy reference, and a couple of blank pages for your own observations, notes, and prayers.

Let's take a few moments now to preview the three main sections of *Put God First*…

Part I: The Quality of Life Defined

Part I explores and offers a working definition for the quality of life. Of course the quality of life has engaged and inspired the genius and imagination of far greater minds than mine over the centuries, so don't be entirely surprised if my humble contribution seems somewhat simple and feebleminded in comparison. Nevertheless, I begin *Part I* by suggesting that the quality of life is defined in large part by how and where and with whom we spend our time, God's first and greatest gift to each of us.

I further suggest that the mechanics of how and where and with whom we spend our time are governed by the rituals that we build around our relationships with everything and everyone in our lives, including and especially God. Rituals – both sacred and profane – dictate how, where and with whom we spend almost every minute of every day; we constantly unfold and consult them like roadmaps to our own lives.

Finally, I suggest that the quality of our lives at any point in time also reflects our proximity to God. During our respective journeys, some of our ritual roadmaps draw us closer to Him while many others lead us farther away...

Part II: The Quality of Life Threatened

Some people are blessed to know from early childhood exactly what they were born to do. My father, for instance, knew from an early age that he wanted to write about baseball. From his lips to God's ear, and so it was. Such, however, was not the case with yours truly, and it took me more than five decades to figure things out for myself. And while I still know abysmally little about what God may have in store for me five minutes from now, I *do* know exactly why He put me here. It turned out to be pretty simple in the end, far simpler in fact than the five decades it took me to figure it out would suggest: He put me here to have faith in Him, and to help Him promote and inspire life-affirming change in others, including *you*. This little book, therefore, is as much His work as it is mine.

So it is with the above disclaimer and license for change that I humbly offer in *Part II* a pair of highly controversial and disquieting assertions: First the claim that obsessive-compulsive behavior and addiction are now *default* conditions in what I call the *Great Age of Mediation*, followed next by the no less disturbing observation that an endemic American *addiction to media* now represents the primary threat to the quality of our personal and institutional lives. Statistically, we now spend *almost all* of our waking time (not to mention a great deal of our money, disposable or otherwise) in fealty to all things media.

Doubtless, many mainstream addiction recovery advocates will take offense to what they read herein, largely because my thoughts refute some of the sacred-cow myths and half-truths that date all the way back to the early days of Alcoholics Anonymous, myths and half-truths that still prevail and dominate today, some seventy years later. I challenge the status quo for a couple of reasons: first, because it is my primary function as a change agent to do so, and second because our reluctance and failure to challenge them prevents us from exploring what may be far more viable alternatives in the *Great Age of Mediation.* We avert our gaze only at our own peril.

You should know, however, that I did not set out initially to challenge mainstream addiction theory. In fact, when I first began to explore the relationship between media and addiction, I was a diehard and enthusiastic 12-step acolyte – like so many other recovering addicts. But the more I studied the relationship between the two, the clearer it became to me that how we perceive our own addictions – including and *especially* our addiction to media – is very much influenced and colored by the addictions themselves. So I was compelled to re-examine my own intellectual and emotional investments en route, and discovered – to my considerable dismay – that they were mired at least as much in popular culture folklore and myth as they were in fact.

That said, those of you who might take exception to my views on addiction should also take heart, because I suspect that you're not alone: I suspect that there will be many media professionals and academicians – especially those who might mistakenly look to the Internet and other digital media as high-tech silver bullets – who join you in your umbrage. Like their counterparts in the addiction recovery industry, media professionals and academicians have their own canon of sacred cows and half-truths to defend, and with almost three decades of senior media industry experience under my belt, I've had plenty of occasion to invoke them all a million times or more.

But *Put God First* is by no one's definition a media industry exposé or critique, nor was that ever my intent. Rather, my primary objective was and remains much more circumscribed: to introduce an alternative explanation for why so many of us find so much deprivation and emptiness amidst such obvious abundance in the *Great Age of Mediation,* and what happens to the quality of our lives and our communities when we do. I would therefore reject any criticism of *Put God First* as anti-media; it's simply not. It is, however, decidedly anti-excess...

In a deliberate manner that some will likely find refreshing and others will just as likely find downright appalling, I cite almost no statistics or research in support of my own bold assertions. In the *Great Age of Mediation* we tend to use statistics as a form of modern numerology to support all manner of things both savory and unsavory, a disturbingly common practice that almost always compromises and sacrifices the truth along the way. Rather, my arguments about both addiction and media – although researched and refined over many years – are forged largely in common sense tempered by almost three decades of personal and professional experience as both an addict and a recognized digital media pioneer.

Some critics will no doubt interpret my lack of statistics as evidence of lazy theories predicated on faith rather than fact. So be it. Far better we should all know sooner rather than later that the wisdom we seek is hidden from the wise and learned. Far better we should know that we are all like children in the eyes of God, and that we walk by our faith, not by our sight. Besides, as a gratefully recovered ex-advertising executive, I'm well prepared and trained to accept faith over fact any day; it pays better and is far more accountable in the end. On a related note, I discovered long ago that only faith gets me out of bed in the morning, and that the facts are typically far too subject to whimsical, partisan, and wholly expedient interpretation by patriots and scoundrels alike. With all due respect, today's newspaper headlines are tomorrow's fish wrap.

For what it's worth, however, I think you'll find my arguments about both addiction and media to be not only sensible and well-reasoned, but invigorating and liberating as well. At least I hope so, though I would encourage you nevertheless to research the numbers and facts yourself to corroborate or refute any of my arguments. If you find something worth noting, please pass it along.

In *Part II* you'll encounter the *Media Log,* an abysmally simple yet supremely challenging exercise designed to expose our own complicity in and capacity for excessive media consumption, our dominant behavioral trait in the *Great Age of Mediation.* You may find the *Media Log* both unsettling and disturbing; many do. Predicated on the essential understanding that we simply can't begin to deal with something

WE SIMPLY CANT BEGIN TO DEAL
WITH SOMETHING THAT WE CANNOT
OR WILL NOT SEE

that we cannot or will not see, the *Media Log* dusts the fingerprints of our unconscious behavior. It renders the invisible visible, and hopefully will motivate a few of us to examine certain behaviors we might otherwise prefer to ignore. The working assumption, however, is that you are reading this book at least in part because you want to explore some new and challenging ideas. You'll find plenty of them in *Part II*.

Finally, you may note far fewer references to God in *Part II* than in *Part I*, no coincidence because *Part II* describes a largely Godless society, one in which we have stationed God dead last in our 21st-century hierarchy of things that matter. In the *Great Age of Mediation*, God is missing from our lives by design; in fact, he wasn't even invited to the party...

[handwritten margin note: GOD PUT LAST]

Part III: The Quality of Life Redeemed

By definition, the *Great Age of Mediation* offers little hope and even less time for the successful application of mainstream addiction recovery platitudes like prevention and abstinence. It's simply far too late to prevent what's already ubiquitous from suddenly showing up; that horse left the barn a long time ago. And it's likely a good thing that all comedy is rooted in tragedy, because the very notion of abstinence in the *Great Age of Mediation* – the age of trillion-dollar consumer economies powered by billions of microchips – borders on laughably quaint, especially in the near-total absence of champions to praise and model the only viable long-term alternative: *moderation.*

All of which begs the following questions: How fortunate are we that our ways are not God's ways? How fortunate are we that God always offers us a better alternative to

[handwritten: Moderation]

our own vanities? How fortunate are we for the daily opportunity to celebrate the many blessings He brings to our lives in the *Great Age of Mediation?*

Part III offers my grateful response to all of the above questions: a proven program to put God first in a gentle daily protocol of conscious intervention predicated on gratitude for the good people and things that contribute to the quality of our lives. *Part III* of *Put God First* teaches us how to interrupt and moderate the extreme influences and harmful thinking – what recovering addicts sometimes refer to as *stinking thinking* – that conspire in the *Great Age of Mediation* to promote profligate consumption, inhibit gratitude, and otherwise diminish the quality of our lives and communities.

Herein you'll find the *human centrifuge,* a compelling graphic model for life in the Great Age of Mediation; it will doubtless make you smile. You'll also find *My Ritual Inventory,* an elegantly simple yet incredibly powerful tool designed to help you put God first in every facet of your life – spiritual, physical, emotional, and social – every day. *My Ritual Inventory* is nothing less than a sheer gratitude engine; it will show you precisely how to invoke God as your personal quality control agent and the primary force for *moderation* in the *Great Age of Mediation*.

Finally, in *Part III* – contrary to the Godless environment of *Part II* – you will find Him almost everywhere you look.

On a personal note...

Put God First is nothing if not proof of the fact that God works in mysterious ways. The mere fact that a devout Muslim pens the preface to a book written by a Born Again Christian with the last name of Einstein is probably proof enough. But what began with broad brushstrokes more than a dozen years ago as separately ambitious studies on technology, media, and addiction eventually merged over time then re-emerged finally – after many surprise permutations, twists and turns – as this modest little book about God and faith and the critical roles they play in the quality of our lives in the *Great Age of Mediation*.

Of course I long ago abandoned any hope or ambition to fathom God's many mysteries (I can't even figure out how to work my universal remote control), and opted more simply in recent years to embrace faith in Him instead. In retrospect, letting go and letting God seems the wiser course; I've since discovered that faith in God has simplified my life and provided an antidote of sorts to the enervating Babel spawned by my own relentless arrogance and self-will run riot over the past few decades. My faith in God has taught me to accept and appreciate the uncertainties and vicissitudes of life as essential components of those things that inspire me most, precisely because those things that now inspire me most never fail to surprise me time and again with the depth and beauty of His reflection in them.

For far too long I've sought control over the people and things around me, only to watch them slip away and elude me, one by one. But I now understand that finding a way to control the events and people in my life was far less important than finding a safe place to let go. <u>*Put God First* is what emerged quite simply when – after many years of struggling with the unmanageable complexities of my own life – I found that place and finally let go.</u>

They say that man makes plans and God laughs. If so, I'm pretty sure that I've kept Him in stitches over the years.

And if so, it seems to me that the very best course of action is to rejoice in Him and with Him, to catch Him when he's in a good mood. Because all things become suddenly possible the very moment we decide to laugh with God. All things become suddenly possible the very moment we put our faith in Him and rejoice, the very moment we realize that He wants only good things for us, only good things for you and for me.

So allow me a brief moment now to express my undying gratitude to Him for the half century and change that it took me to get here. Despite my many character flaws, I remain thoroughly delighted, amused and bemused by the fact that I've circled the block a thousand times only to find myself still very much in love with the promise of redemption.

God is great, and finding Him in my early fifties (what He was doing in my early fifties I'll never know) likely had much to do with my renewed interest in redemption. So too did the birth of my only child, a precious little girl, just a few years earlier. In her I rediscover God's eternal love for me each and every day. I suspect that the confluence of these two wondrous gifts so late in my life combined with the somewhat less wonderful but liberating collapse of my digital marketing career shortly thereafter to set my current course and seal my fate. *Put God First* is just partial testimony to what a long strange trip it's been.

For me, however, redemption has always been and still remains an ongoing process, always long in coming and always hard-earned. I became a Born Again Christian not because – as some religious scholars and critics may argue – it's an easy or convenient conversion (it was neither for me), but because the Holy Spirit entered my soul one day and because I suddenly found in the Good News a much more *rational* and meaningful approach to life in the *Great Age of Mediation,* my old home address. Life simply makes more sense when I put God first.

Put God First reflects much of what I have learned on my personal journey to redemption, and I offer it now to you as a step-by-step guide to a better, richer, more integrated life as we continue on our individual and collective sojourns through the *Great Age of Mediation.* I can unconditionally promise and guarantee no shortcuts en route, and would suggest that you hold on to your wallet if and when you encounter someone who promises otherwise. Make no mistake: God moves mountains, but you and I are better advised to bring our own shovels.

I tell my little girl to approach everything always with three priceless treasures in hand: gratitude, enthusiasm, and patience – the exact same qualities that both God and she never fail to inspire and demand in me. Thus am I exceedingly grateful, and *always* ready to rally. As for patience: Let's you and I agree to meet across the river on the other side in the Promised Land.

Until then maybe our paths will cross someday; I'd like that. Or maybe we'll meet online; I'm pretty visible.

Finally, thank you so much for buying my book, and please be sure to tell a friend or loved one about it. Despite the politically incorrect tarnish accrued by evangelism in recent years, common sense is common sense, and if you can't bring yourself for whatever reason to spread the Good

News, at least spread a little common sense. Meanwhile, travel safe and always put God first…

Jeff Einstein – October, 2007

Part I

The Quality of Life
Defined

Chapter 1
The quality of life as a function of time...

Dear God,

Thank you for the gift of time and the many other gifts you give me. Thank you for the meaning your unconditional love brings to my life. Please help me appreciate and praise you for all of the good things you fashion for me. Show me what is good. Help me recognize and pursue quality in your name forever. Lord, hear my prayer. Amen.

God shows us what is good. Personally, however, I find it difficult to *define* quality, although I typically know it when I *encounter* it; most quality things simply stand out from their less quality counterparts. They seem to command and reveal more reverence for and attention to detail, even a greater appreciation for the very time and space they occupy. Quality almost always surprises me when I find it, no matter how much I expect or anticipate it. Yet it doesn't seem to matter what form quality assumes or where I find it; regardless, an encounter with quality always makes me feel good and happy to be alive. I thank God for a good meal. I thank God for a good book, or a good piece of music. I thank God for a beautiful spring day and my little girl's smile. I thank God for you, dear reader. All of which leads me to conclude quite simply that quality is God-given.

QUALITY IS GOD-GIVEN.

God gives us life and fills it with good things. He creates and recreates us daily. He renders us from darkness and void, and breathes life into us. While we can certainly aspire to the knowledge of God (at our own considerable risk), we simply cannot know with any measure of real certainty what awaits us from moment to moment, so we proceed in faith instead, burdened by our own mortality and a glaring lack of viable alternatives. Truly, there but for the grace of God go each and every one of us, every minute of every day. The fact that we all concede this (at least privately to ourselves) each time we confront a humbling moment in our lives indicates that we also know and concede that quality imparts meaning...

QUALITY IMPARTS MEANING.

While we cannot know with certainty what awaits us just around the next bend, we can nevertheless sleep securely wrapped in the blanket of God's unconditional love for us. His love brings meaning to our lives; without it there is no meaning and all is vanity. The quality we encounter in our lives is nothing less than a reflection of God's love for us. He fills our lives with good things so we can know the textures, colors, shapes, scents, flavors, and inspiration in their goodness, know Him better through them, and lead better *quality* lives through Him. The many good things in our lives – some of which seem to come to us in spite of ourselves – simply confirm that we're not the only ones working on our own behalf.

Of course talk is cheap, and in the end our appreciation for all of the good things God gives us is measured in the amount of time and attention that we actually lavish on them, and – more important – on the amount of time and attention that we lavish on Him.

QUALITY REQUIRES TIME AND ATTENTION.

5

Time of course is our most precious inventory. Time on this earth is our first and most valuable God-given gift, a blessing that only He can bestow and only He can rescind. Of all the precious gifts He gives us, time is the only one we cannot replenish, the only one we cannot replace. We can replenish our faith, replenish our health, replenish our money, and sometimes even redeem and replenish abused trust. But once our time is gone, it's gone forever, never to return.

TIME IS OUR MOST PRECIOUS INVENTORY.

Time in the *Great Age of Mediation*, however, seems to be in pretty short supply. Chronic time starvation is the most frequent and ubiquitous complaint of modern life; it's the default condition from which rises the 21st century's most common and predictable refrain: *"If only I had more time."*

We are forever complaining about the dearth of time in our lives: "Not enough time to spend with my spouse. Not enough time to spend with my kids. Not enough time to spend with my friends. Not enough time to spend with my hobbies. Not enough down time, not enough up time, not enough quality time." The litany of things we simply don't have time for anymore seems to stretch on forever. Unfortunately, in the *Great Age of Mediation*, God is most likely one of those things. In fact, He's likely near the top of the list of things that we simply don't have time for anymore.

Ironically, we are so consumed by our own perception of chronic time deprivation that we devote hours each week to prioritizing our schedules, when we would probably be much better advised to take just a few minutes each day to re-examine and schedule our priorities instead – per the pithy title of lifestyle guru Stephen Covey's book, *First Things First*. We will learn how to put God first in our lives only when we learn how to schedule our priorities *before* we try to manage our time. Clearly, however, we have some important choices to make.

WE SHOULD SCHEDULE OUR PRIORITIES INSTEAD OF PRIORITIZING OUR SCHEDULES.

Yet how, one might ask, is it even remotely possible to exhaust our most precious resource in the *Great Age of Mediation*? How can we run out of time when we are so utterly immersed in and consumed with so much *time-saving* technology? I once added up all of the time I've spent in the past 25 years just rebooting my PC. Admittedly, I'm a power user, but I predicated my calculations nevertheless on a *conservative* estimate of two reboots every weekday, at three minutes per reboot. The numbers follow...

2 reboots x 3 minutes/reboot x 5 days/week
= 30 minutes/week
X 50 weeks (two weeks off)
= 1,500 min/year
= 25 hours/year
x 25 years
= 625 hours
= 26 days

Almost *an entire month of my life* dedicated exclusively to watching my computer reboot – and that doesn't even include the considerable time spent trying to diagnose what went wrong each time. But that's just the tip of the proverbial iceberg: How much time do you spend on the phone each month with customer support folks? How much time do you spend waiting at home for service technicians to show up? How much time do you spend each month trying to figure out why your latest user-friendly digital gadget doesn't seem to work for you the way it does in the TV ads? The point behind all of these rhetorical questions is almost painfully transparent: The excess that defines the *Great Age of Mediation* almost always sneaks up on us. And it all takes time, the one thing we can't manufacture more of.

EXCESS SNEAKS UP ON US.

We behave, however, as if chronic time starvation is somehow ordained by God. But it's not, not in this or any other era. God determines only the dates that we enter and exit this life. Exactly how we choose to spend the time between those dates, however, is purely up to us.

Nevertheless, we predicate our behavior on our perceptions, not on our realities, and we *perceive* ourselves as chronically time-starved, so we *behave* accordingly. But how does the *perception* of chronic time deprivation change our *behavior?* How do we assess the loss of time in our lives, how do we respond to the loss, and what do we sacrifice in the process?

I suggest that what we most fear losing, what we feel slipping inexorably away from us in the *Great Age of Mediation*, is the very quality of our lives, no matter how we define it. We fear losing our families, we fear losing our homes, we fear losing our incomes, we fear losing our freedoms, we fear losing our reputations, and we even fear losing our minds. We fear the loss of *quality* things in our lives because we've already lost what's most important to us: our faith in God. So we compensate with *quantity* instead. Thus the *perception* of deprivation drives the *reality* of excess.

A Native American shaman once explained to me his theory for why European Americans are so enthralled with houseplants. "It's because you fear the loss," he told me. "It's because of the distance you place between yourself and your own God. When the autumn leaves turn brown and fall from the trees in preparation for winter, you no longer believe in your heart of hearts that the Great Spirit will return and renew the green in the springtime. Instead, you gather all of the potted green you can and bring it into your home. You horde the green so you won't feel the loss." The real loss in the shaman's allegory of course had nothing to do with houseplants. He was talking about the loss of faith and the corresponding replacement of quality with quantity.

En route from deprivation to excess, however, our fear of loss prevents us from taking the time to appreciate and attend to the good things in life. We're much too busy it seems just circling the wagons. But we cannot hope to recognize the quality in something that we simply won't take the time to appreciate. The more fearful we become, the less inclined we are to create time in our already impossible schedules to appreciate and attend to all of the wonderful people and things in our lives. And the less time we take to appreciate and attend to all of the wonderful people and things in our lives, the easier it becomes to neglect or dismiss them the next time we run short on time. The more practiced and efficient we become at neglect for the good people and things around us, the harder it becomes to see the Hand of God at work in our lives. Appreciation is a conscious act of *commission*; it always precedes the recognition of quality, and it requires practice. Appreciation – like excess – takes time.

> **APPRECIATION IS A CONSCIOUS ACT OF COMMISSION. APPRECIATION ALWAYS PRECEDES THE RECOGNITION OF QUALITY.**

Unfortunately, it's difficult to sustain an environment that will support both appreciation and excess. We simply don't have the time to entertain both. Consequently, we begin to lose our ability to recognize quality in others the very moment we stop investing the time to look for and appreciate it in our own lives, the very moment we begin to value quantity over quality. Again, we simply cannot expect to recognize quality in what we do not take the time to appreciate, including and especially our relationship with God. We cannot fully know Him until we appreciate and worship Him first, until we choose to put first things first. Orphaned in the mad rush and cacophony of our technocratic lifestyles, our relationship with God withers from neglect. Our faith in

10

Him is the first and greatest casualty of perceived time deprivation.

> **WE LOSE OUR ABILITY TO RECOGNIZE QUALITY IN OTHERS WHEN WE STOP INVESTING THE TIME TO LOOK FOR AND APPRECIATE IT IN OUR OWN LIVES.**

No, we can't control what God will or won't give us, nor can we control which cards He will or won't deal us throughout our lives. But we can, however, determine how we spend the time He gives us, because among His many gifts to us is *free will*. Even the most diehard addict chooses the daily behaviors that raise the prison bars of his addiction. Yet the same diehard addict can choose behaviors that will lower those same bars. Such small miracles occur millions of times each and every day. The difference between an addict and a recovered addict, like the difference between bear and bull markets, is faith. Likewise, the active presence of God in our lives – like our ability to appreciate and recognize quality – is a conscious act of commission, an act of choice, an act of free will. Most of all, however, God's presence in our lives is an act of faith.

> **THE ACTIVE PRESENCE OF GOD IN OUR LIVES IS A CONSCIOUS ACT OF COMMISSION.**

On further examination, therefore, we begin to notice that the quality of life is an essential function of time and faith. More specifically, we begin to see the quality of life as a reflection of how and where and with whom we choose to spend our time.

THE QUALITY OF LIFE IS A REFLECTION OF HOW AND WHERE AND WITH WHOM WE CHOOSE TO SPEND OUR TIME.

Chapter 1 Summary

QUALITY IS GOD-GIVEN.

QUALITY IMPARTS MEANING.

QUALITY REQUIRES TIME AND ATTENTION.

TIME IS OUR MOST PRECIOUS INVENTORY.

WE SHOULD SCHEDULE OUR PRIORITIES INSTEAD OF PRIORITIZING OUR SCHEDULES.

EXCESS SNEAKS UP ON US.

APPRECIATION IS A CONSCIOUS ACT OF COMMISSION.

APPRECIATION ALWAYS PRECEDES THE RECOGNITION OF QUALITY.

WE LOSE OUR ABILITY TO RECOGNIZE QUALITY IN OTHERS WHEN WE STOP INVESTING THE TIME TO LOOK FOR AND APPRECIATE IT IN OUR OWN LIVES.

THE ACTIVE PRESENCE OF GOD IN OUR LIVES IS A CONSCIOUS ACT OF COMMISSION.

Chapter 1 Summary (cont'd)

**THE QUALITY OF LIFE IS A REFLECTION
OF HOW AND WHERE AND WITH WHOM
WE CHOOSE TO SPEND OUR TIME.**

My Notes

My Notes

Chapter 2
Ritual: Arbiter of time…

Dear God,

Thank you for filling my life with so many good things for me to care for and attend to. Help me spend my time in fealty and service to you and the good things you bestow upon me. Draw me closer to you, and help me avoid those things that distance me from you. Lord, walk with me today. Amen.

If the quality of our lives reflects how and where and with whom we choose to spend our time, then it makes sense to examine the actual mechanics of how and where and with whom we choose to spend it. How do we parcel the time God gives us, and what structures do we erect around it to guide and arbitrate the choices we make about how and where and with whom we choose to spend it? How do the mechanics of how and where and with whom we choose to spend our time in the *Great Age of Mediation* actually work?

With all due respect to fundamental Creationist theory, Darwin had it right – only backwards. Instead of evolving *from* apes, we're involving *into* apes. With any luck, in another fifty million years we might find ourselves sitting high atop the jungle canopy with a magnificent view and a delightful fruit platter. I project this whimsy because it occurs to me that – while we may prefer to think of ourselves as rational actors on a rational stage in an enlightened postmodern world – the actual mechanics of how, where and with whom we spend our time haven't changed much since the early days of tribal civilization. We've always invested our time pretty much the same way: in pursuit of the many and varied relationships that in aggregate constitute the fabrics of our lives. We have relationships with God, relationships with family, relationships with other people, relationships with authority, relationships with the earth and the other species that populate it, relationships with community, relationships with work, relationships with money, relationships with food, relationships with our bodies, relationships with institutions, relationships with art, relationships with our passions, relationships with our toys, relationships with our creditors, relationships with our technologies, and relationships with our obsessions and addictions. Life is an increasingly complex tapestry of interwoven relationships, each of which – for better or worse – demands a measure of our time and attention.

WE SPEND ALL OF OUR TIME IN VARIOUS RELATIONSHIPS OF ALL KINDS.

Whatever value our relationships accrue in our lives is assigned to them when we decide how much time and attention they require or deserve. We simply devote more time and attention to relationships with those things and people that we deem more important to us for whatever reason. We enter into some relationships by choice; others are sometimes thrust upon us by a confluence of circumstance or the inevitable riptide of protracted neglect. The amount of time and attention we devote to the relationships in our lives may change with circumstance, but our investments in time and attention always reveal current snapshots of our deepest values en route. Our investments in time and attention always expose the hierarchy of our priorities to the bone. We cannot hide from ourselves, and we certainly can't hide from God. What was important to us yesterday may be less so today, and today's afterthought may be tomorrow's headline, but you can pretty much rest assured that your current values are a reflection of how and where you invest your time and attention, and vice versa: how and where you invest your time and attention will reflect your values.

> **WE ASSIGN VALUE TO OUR RELATIONSHIPS WHEN WE DECIDE HOW MUCH TIME AND ATTENTION TO DEVOTE TO THEM.**

> **HOW AND WHERE WE INVEST OUR TIME AND ATTENTION REFLECTS OUR VALUES.**

Once the decision is made to invest in a relationship, the mechanics of that investment are governed by the *rituals* we build to service it. How and where and with whom we spend our time, therefore, is governed by the rituals we build to service each of our many relationships.

> **HOW WE SPEND OUR TIME IS GOVERNED BY THE RITUALS WE BUILD TO SERVICE OUR RELATIONSHIPS.**

Simply defined, rituals are routinely scheduled activities that we erect to service and facilitate our relationships with other people and things, our relationship with God not least; they govern *exactly* how we spend our time. We devise and deploy rituals to cover each and every relationship *in* and virtually every minute *of* our lives. Rituals govern what we

do when we wake up in the morning, how we get to work, what we do and how we perform at work, how and when we get home, what we do when we get there, and how we retire for the night. Clearly, our rituals determine how and where and with whom we choose to spend our time.

But not all rituals impart the same value or function the same way. As arbiters of quality, the rituals in our lives can be classified as either *self-serving* or *meaningful*. Self-serving rituals are those we devise and erect in fealty to our obsessions and addictions. They reflect only our own narcissism and fears, and cannot by definition be invoked to help ourselves or anyone else. Self-serving rituals are essentially toxic; they typically value quantity over quality, promote excess over moderation, convenience over ethics, and the perception of deprivation over abundance. Reactive by nature, they insert distance between us and God. By contrast, meaningful rituals are those we devise and erect to enhance and promote our own spiritual, physical, emotional, and social wellbeing, and the spiritual, physical, emotional, and social wellbeing of others. Meaningful rituals typically value quality over quantity, promote moderation over excess, ethics over convenience, and abundance over the perception of deprivation. Proactive by nature, they draw us closer to God.

The table below lists and compares the respective attributes of both self-serving and meaningful ritual:

Self-Serving	Meaningful
• promote obsession	• promote moderation
• promote quantity	• promote quality
• promote convenience	• promote ethics
• are reactive	• are proactive
• promote deprivation	• promote abundance
• distance us from God	• draw us closer to God

Many recovery experts describe addiction as ritualized obsessive-compulsive behavior. As such, self-serving ritual actually promotes and facilitates our addictions. In fact, every one of our addictions – from cigarettes to gambling – is immersed *in* and defined *by* self-serving ritual. But if self-serving ritual facilitates and promotes our obsessions and addictions, what practical functions does meaningful ritual provide for us? I'm glad you asked; let's make a list...

Meaningful ritual brings structure to our lives

In the act of structuring our time, ritual imposes structure on our lives as well. The importance of structure in our lives is reflected in the fact that just before Moses ascended Mt. Sinai to receive the Ten Commandments from God, he met with his wife's father, Jethro, in whom he confided the burdens of leadership that weighed so heavily upon him. A wise and patient man, Jethro offered his weary son-in-law a much more efficient system to help him adjudicate disputes among the Israelites. So as it turned out, even before God's Holy Law was passed down to Moses, a structure was created to ensure its fidelity and faithful application.

Simply stated, structure is where the rubber hits the road in our lives. Anyone who suddenly loses a job will tell you just how difficult and daunting it is to restructure their time from scratch each and every morning. In fact, anyone who even lives with someone who loses a job will testify to the massive disruption imposed by the sudden loss of structure. It's one of the major reasons why we feel so awkward on the first day or two of every vacation; we suddenly find ourselves away from our familiar support structures and all of the comforting accoutrements that ride shotgun with them. It's why the greatest perceived enemy of Western civilization is anarchy.

MEANINGFUL RITUAL BRINGS STRUCTURE TO OUR LIVES.

Meaningful ritual brings context and continuity to our lives

Meaningful ritual is much more than just a convenient way to structure our time. Meaningful ritual is how we structure and ascribe value and meaning to the mundane and commonplace things and events in our lives; each ritualized structure we erect comes replete with its own unique suite of colors and textures and tastes and sounds and emotions. Granted, brushing your teeth every morning likely won't win you any awards, but it's an integral part of the same morning ritual that includes waking up on time, breakfast, getting the kids off to school, and making your way to work – all essential components to the quality of your life. All meaningful ritual provides structure, and structure sculpts the topography, the hills and valleys, the *contexts* of our lives. Beyond context, however, looms the very real need for *continuity.* As creatures of faith first and foremost we *need* to know in our heart of hearts that the sun will rise in the morning and set in the evening; we *need* to know that the green will return in the spring. Despite our sometimes frantic efforts to escape our pasts, we *need* the attachment to what was in order to bring meaning and perspective to what is and what will be.

> **MEANINGFUL RITUAL PROVIDES CONTEXT AND CONTINUITY IN OUR LIVES.**

Meaningful ritual provides social and religious infrastructure in our lives

All of our social and religious institutions are full of meaningful ritual. It informs our behavior in every courtroom, in every classroom, in every corporate boardroom, and in every single church, synagogue, and mosque on the planet. It guides our interactions with others and with God, and tells us what we can reasonably expect from them in return. Meaningful ritual helps us safely reach outside ourselves in a spirit of generosity and compassion; it's well-documented and no accident that local churches and religious institutions are typically far more effective at providing emergency relief and community services than their better-funded government and secular NGO counterparts. Meaningful ritual is how we carve out and sustain a place for God in our lives.

> **MEANINGFUL RITUAL PROVIDES SOCIAL AND RELIGIOUS INFRASTRUCTURE IN OUR LIVES.**

Meaningful ritual makes us more conscious and less self-conscious

Meaningful ritual is detail-intensive; it slows us down and compels us to pay attention to the little things in life. Doing so simply makes us more conscious of the world around us, and less self-conscious, less self-absorbed – probably not a bad thing in a society otherwise benumbed by endemic narcissistic narcosis, an endless fascination with our own reflections. Moreover, as you'll learn later, a good deal of the meaningful ritual in our lives is socially attuned, and relies explicitly on our abilities to cultivate and sustain relationships with other individuals and institutions. Through them we learn not only how the behaviors of others affect our lives, but how our behavior affects others as well.

> **MEANINGFUL RITUAL MAKES US MORE CONSCIOUS OF THE WORLD AROUND US AND LESS SELF-CONSCIOUS.**

25

Meaningful ritual makes us accountable

In the *Great Age of Mediation* there can be no accountability unless and until we are first and foremost accountable to God. Despite the alarmist claims of secularists and atheists alike, we *are* in fact *one nation under God* irrespective of our critically important and inspired separation of church and state. God is emblazoned on our money and carved into our courtrooms and legislative chambers for a reason; He is found in virtually every public institution for a reason: not only as a reflection of our faith in Him, but because we *require* an ultimate authority in our lives. Otherwise, there is no ultimate truth, and all arguments – from saints and sinners alike – are equally valid. And where there is no truth, wherever all truth is rendered relative by man, there can be *no* accountability to God – or to anyone else.

MEANINGFUL RITUAL MAKES US ACCOUNTABLE.

Meaningful ritual reminds us that there is indeed an ultimate authority, a power far greater than ourselves, and a truth that lies far above and beyond any we might fashion for ourselves. Meaningful ritual holds us accountable to God and His creations.

Without meaningful ritual in our lives we would be utterly lost and forsaken. Their absence would paralyze us in a heartbeat. Also important to the overall quality of our lives, therefore, is the ratio of self-serving versus meaningful ritual. In general, the more we fill our lives with self-serving ritual, the less quality of life we will enjoy, whereas more meaningful ritual will generally result in better overall quality of life – at least as defined by the above table of attributes.

The same ratio of self-serving to meaningful ritual also determines our relative distance from God at any given point in time. The more we occupy our time with self-serving ritual, the more we distance ourselves from God. Conversely, the more we occupy our time with meaningful ritual, the closer we draw ourselves towards God. It's also important to note that God *always* wants to draw us near. If there is distance between us and Him, it's only because *we* put it there.

SELF-SERVING RITUAL PUTS DISTANCE BETWEEN US AND GOD. MEANINGFUL RITUAL DRAWS US CLOSER TO GOD.

GOD ALWAYS WANTS US TO DRAW NEARER TO HIM.

Finally, therefore, we can conclude that the quality of our lives reflects the ratio of self-serving versus meaningful ritual in our lives, and – ultimately – the amount of distance that we place between ourselves and God.

THE QUALITY OF OUR LIVES REFLECTS
THE RATIO OF SELF-SERVING VERSUS
MEANINGFUL RITUAL IN OUR LIVES, AND
— ULTIMATELY — THE DISTANCE WE
PLACE BETWEEN OURSELVES AND GOD.

Chapter 2 Summary

WE SPEND ALL OF OUR TIME IN VARIOUS RELATIONSHIPS OF ALL KINDS.

WE ASSIGN VALUE TO OUR RELATIONSHIPS WHEN WE DECIDE HOW MUCH TIME AND ATTENTION TO DEVOTE TO THEM.

HOW AND WHERE WE INVEST OUR TIME AND ATTENTION REFLECTS OUR VALUES.

HOW WE SPEND OUR TIME IS GOVERNED BY THE RITUALS WE BUILD TO SERVICE OUR RELATIONSHIPS.

MEANINGFUL RITUAL BRINGS STRUCTURE TO OUR LIVES.

MEANINGFUL RITUAL PROVIDES CONTEXT AND CONTINUITY IN OUR LIVES.

MEANINGFUL RITUAL PROVIDES SOCIAL AND RELIGIOUS INFRASTRUCTURE IN OUR LIVES.

MEANINGFUL RITUAL MAKES US MORE CONSCIOUS OF THE WORLD AROUND US AND LESS SELF-CONSCIOUS.

Chapter 2 Summary (cont'd)

MEANINGFUL RITUAL MAKES US
ACCOUNTABLE.

SELF-SERVING RITUAL PUTS DISTANCE
BETWEEN US AND GOD. MEANINGFUL
RITUAL DRAWS US CLOSER TO GOD.

GOD ALWAYS WANTS US TO DRAW
NEARER TO HIM.

THE QUALITY OF OUR LIVES REFLECTS
THE RATIO OF SELF-SERVING VERSUS
MEANINGFUL RITUAL IN OUR LIVES,
AND —ULTIMATELY — THE DISTANCE WE
PLACE BETWEEN OURSELVES AND GOD.

My Notes

My Notes

Part II

The Quality of Life
Threatened

Chapter 3
Eat all you want, we'll make more...

Dear God,

Thank you for creating me amidst such abundance. Thank you for your favor, and thank you for filling my life with so many good things. Please help me distinguish between those things that glorify you and help me from those that defile you and hurt me. Please forgive me when I confuse them, Lord, and guide me in the choices I make today. Your divine will be done. Amen.

"The paradox of our time in history is that we have taller buildings but shorter tempers, wider freeways, but narrower viewpoints. We spend more, but have less, we buy more, but enjoy less. We have bigger houses and smaller families, more conveniences, but less time. We have more degrees but less sense, more knowledge, but less judgment, more experts, yet more problems, more medicine, but less wellness.

"We drink too much, smoke too much, spend too recklessly, laugh too little, drive too fast, get too angry, stay up too late, get up too tired, read too little, watch TV too much, and pray too seldom. We have multiplied our possessions, but reduced our values. We talk too much, love too seldom, and hate too often.

"We've learned how to make a living, but not a life. We've added years to life not life to years. We've been all the way to the moon and back, but have trouble crossing the street to meet a new neighbor. We conquered outer space but not inner space. We've done larger things, but not better things.

"We've cleaned up the air, but polluted the soul. We've conquered the atom, but not our prejudice. We write more, but learn less. We plan more, but accomplish less. We've learned to rush, but not to wait. We build more computers to hold more information, to produce more copies than ever, but we communicate less and less.

"These are the times of fast foods and slow digestion, big men and small character, steep profits and shallow re-lationships. These are the days of two incomes but more divorce, fancier houses, but broken homes. These are days of quick trips, disposable diapers, throwaway morality,

one night stands, overweight bodies, and pills that do eve-rything from cheer, to quiet, to kill. It is a time when there is much in the showroom window and nothing in the stockroom. A time when technology can bring this letter to you, and a time when you can choose either to share this insight, or to just hit delete..."
- George Carlin

We live in extraordinary times. Less than a generation ago, addiction was the exception. But no longer. In recent years – concurrent with the massive explosion of digital bandwidth in the mid-1990s – obsessive-compulsive behavior and addiction have become the undisputed *rule*. Obsessive-compulsive behavior and addiction now represent nothing less than business as usual in the *Great Age of Mediation*. Witness *millions* of alcoholics, *millions* of sex addicts, *tens of millions* of food addicts, *tens of millions* of nicotine addicts, *millions* of licit and illicit drug addicts, and *millions upon millions* more compulsive gamblers, workaholics, and shopaholics. Witness addicts in the bedroom, addicts in the classroom, addicts in the boardroom, addicts in the courtroom, and addicts in the locker room. It seems as if we just can't throw a brick nowadays and not hit an addict. Sometimes it seems as if we are all born as crack babies in the *Great Age of Mediation*.

> **IN THE *GREAT AGE OF MEDIATION*, OBSESSIVE-COMPULSIVE BEHAVIOR AND ADDICTION ARE NO LONGER THE EXCEPTION. THEY ARE THE RULE.**

I know it sounds outrageous, and I certainly don't mean to offend anyone, but think about it: How many of us can claim a life devoid of obsessive-compulsive behavior or addiction? Who do you know whose life hasn't been touched directly or indirectly by *at least one* of the above addictions at one time or another? And given the already extensive and ever-expanding litany of recognized addictions in American society, it seems perfectly obvious that we can and often do become addicted to just about any experience that offers us the promise of reliable pleasure and relief over and over again.

In fact, the more you look around, the less outrageous my default addiction theory sounds. The truth is that almost all of us have engaged in various compulsive behaviors or addictions at various times in our lives (and as you'll see in the very next chapter, *the vast majority* of us still do).

Of course some compulsive behaviors and addictions are simply more debilitating and disruptive than others, and most don't travel solo; as one might expect, most obsessive-compulsive behaviors and addictions accompany other compulsive behaviors and addictions. Anyone who has ever attended an AA meeting will testify to the rampant presence of cigarettes and coffee, just as anyone who has ever entered a casino will testify to clouds of cigarette smoke and squadrons of cocktail waitresses.

> **WE CAN AND OFTEN DO BECOME
> ADDICTED TO JUST ABOUT ANY
> EXPERIENCE THAT OFFERS US THE
> PROMISE OF RELIABLE PLEASURE AND
> RELIEF OVER AND OVER AGAIN.**

Search the Internet and you'll find a long litany of medical, pharmacological, and psychological definitions for addiction (mostly from organizations with patently self-serving agendas). Almost every definition of addiction you find, however, is a variation on one of two basic themes:

1. By far the more dominant definition of addiction – the one adopted by most healthcare professionals and rehab programs (including all 12-step programs) – describes it as an incurable, chronic, progressive and ultimately fatal disease that requires nothing less than immediate medical and/or peer intervention.

2. A small but quite vocal minority, however, defines addiction as a common and largely self-correcting lifestyle coping mechanism gone awry. Addiction, they argue, comes and goes in our lives depending in large part on circumstance.

Basically, the addiction-as-disease advocates argue that addicts are victimized by their addictions *in spite* of their values, while those who view addiction as a lifestyle coping mechanism gone awry argue that addicts are complicit in their addictions *because* of their values. Typically, those who advocate the addiction-as-disease model embrace *abstinence* while those who consider addiction a lifestyle coping mechanism eschew abstinence and champion *moderation* instead.

My personal experience with and observations of addiction over the past few decades have left me with a few conclusions: First, that addiction is in fact a lifestyle coping mechanism gone awry, not a disease. Next, that addiction travels *laterally* in our lives; it's like an inner tube in the water: Press down on it in one place, and it likely pops up somewhere else. Finally, I think the root cause of addiction is less physical, less pharmacological, less emotional, and more *spiritual*. I think we turn to addiction to compensate for our spiritual emptiness, for the loss of faith mentioned in the shaman's story earlier. I think we turn increasingly *towards* addiction as we turn increasingly – in the *Great Age of Mediation – away* from God. Addiction is a flight from God, a flight and respite from personal accountability.

**THE ROOT CAUSE OF ADDICTION IS
LESS PHYSICAL,
LESS PHARMACOLOGICAL,
LESS EMOTIONAL,
AND MORE SPIRITUAL.**

**WE TURN TO ADDICTION TO
COMPENSATE FOR OUR SPIRITUAL
EMPTINESS.**

**WE TURN INCREASINGLY TOWARDS
ADDICTION AS WE TURN INCREASINGLY
AWAY FROM GOD.**

**ADDICTION IS A FLIGHT FROM GOD, A
FLIGHT AND RESPITE FROM PERSONAL
RESPONSIBILITY.**

And therein lurks the true hidden cost of obsessive-compulsive behavior and addiction: Time devoted to our obsessions and addictions is time diverted *away* from the quality of life. As we turn away from God in fealty to our obsessions and addictions, we forsake the opportunity to know Him better. We forsake the opportunity to know and love ourselves as He knows and loves us. We forsake the *quality* and *meaning* that He offers us in spite of ourselves.

**TIME DEVOTED TO OUR OBSESSIONS
AND ADDICTIONS IS TIME DIVERTED
AWAY FROM THE QUALITY OF LIFE.**

41

Chapter 3 Summary

IN THE *GREAT AGE OF MEDIATION*,
OBSESSIVE-COMPULSIVE BEHAVIOR AND
ADDICTION ARE NO LONGER THE
EXCEPTION. THEY ARE THE RULE.

WE CAN AND OFTEN DO BECOME
ADDICTED TO JUST ABOUT ANY
EXPERIENCE THAT OFFERS US THE
PROMISE OF RELIABLE PLEASURE AND
RELIEF OVER AND OVER AGAIN.

THE ROOT CAUSE OF ADDICTION IS
LESS PHYSICAL,
LESS PHARMACOLOGICAL,
LESS EMOTIONAL,
AND MORE SPIRITUAL.

WE TURN TO ADDICTION TO
COMPENSATE FOR OUR SPIRITUAL
EMPTINESS.

WE TURN INCREASINGLY TOWARDS
ADDICTION AS WE TURN INCREASINGLY
AWAY FROM GOD.

ADDICTION IS A FLIGHT FROM GOD, A
FLIGHT AND RESPITE FROM PERSONAL
RESPONSIBILITY.

TIME DEVOTED TO OUR OBSESSIONS
AND ADDICTIONS IS TIME DIVERTED
AWAY FROM THE QUALITY OF LIFE.

My Notes

My Notes

Chapter 4
If it looks like a duck...

Dear God,

Thank you for giving me thought and language to express myself. Thank you for giving me the tools and technologies to communicate. Thank you for giving me eyes to see and ears to hear. Thank you for the passion you breathe into me. Help me use the gifts you give me wisely and humbly. Help me use them to spread your word. Help me become an instrument of your divine will and carry your message wherever I go. Amen.

ADDICTION

For all of the passion that the topic of addiction – of how we cope with excess in the *Great Age of Mediation* – understandably invokes in us, we shouldn't fool ourselves: We can argue the definition of addiction *ad nauseum,* but in the end it doesn't matter much which one we adopt, because in the end what makes us addicts has less to do with how we *define* addiction and more to do with how we *diagnose* it.

While our respective definitions of addiction may vary, the *diagnosis* of addiction remains a model of consistency. We almost always predicate our diagnosis of addiction on the exact same criteria, on the exact same elemental observation: the amount of *time* and *money* an addict invests in the procurement and consumption of his or her favorite drug(s).

> **ADDICTION IS ALMOST ALWAYS DIAGNOSED AS A MEASURE OF HOW MUCH TIME AND MONEY THE ADDICT DEVOTES TO HIS OR HER FAVORITE DRUG(S).**

The drug itself, however, is incidental; it can be anything: heroin or sex, cocaine or gambling, cigarettes or easy credit, uppers or downers, or any combination of the above. It can be just about anything because contrary to the popular misconception, addiction is *never* about the specific drug. Rather, it's about *behavior.* It's about how we spend our time and money.

ADDICTION IS NEVER ABOUT THE
SPECIFIC DRUG. RATHER, IT'S ABOUT
BEHAVIOR. IT'S ABOUT HOW WE SPEND
OUR TIME AND MONEY.

If, however, the diagnosis of addiction is predicated on the amount of time and money we invest in our favorite drug(s), what constitutes too much? Where do we draw the line that separates obsession from addiction? How much time is too much time? How much money is too much money? After all, what may look like a lot of money to you or me may be pocket change to someone else. And some folks undoubtedly have more discretionary time than others. True, we may and typically do draw the line in different places, but I rather think that addiction is kind of like pornography: We usually know it when we see it (especially when we see it in someone else), which may explain why it's *far more likely* for your spouse or boss or sibling or friend to diagnose you as a compulsive gambler, sex addict, or alcoholic than your doctor. Indeed, addiction is *almost always* a lay diagnosis, at least initially. After all, your doctor probably doesn't know very much about how you spend your time or where you spend your money. And if your spouse doesn't already know, it's probably only a matter of time before he or she finds out. In other words: *If it looks like a duck...*

Now consider: According to the 2004 *Middletown Media Studies,* the first large-scale *observational* study of American media consumption, the average American adult consumes

47

11.7 hours of media each and every day. That's *4,270 hours* per year of media consumption, almost *half a year* of media consumption for each and every year of our adult lives. Seems to me that we crossed the line that separates our obsession *with* media from an addiction *to* media some time ago, and that we haven't bothered to look back since. What's almost as astonishing as the amount of media we consume is the very idea that we somehow accept or view it as *reasonable* (or at least as not unreasonable). But if that's the case, how much is too much? If almost twelve hours of media consumption each and every day is *reasonable,* how much is *unreasonable?*

> ### THE AVERAGE AMERICAN ADULT CONSUMES 11.7 HOURS OF MEDIA EACH AND EVERY DAY.

As with most things, the more media we consume, the more we pay. Like most other commodities (and narcotics), the price of media usually increases relative to the demand. For instance, just a single generation ago (when average media consumption was only about a third of what it is today), most Americans still watched broadcast TV for free. Now, however, almost all Americans are wired for cable, and the average cable TV bill has increased by more than *90 percent* over the past decade alone. Of course nowadays there simply is no more "free" TV to speak of, and soon there won't be any more "free" radio either. Likewise, our monthly ISP bills – which we now take for granted but just ten years ago didn't exist at all for most of us – have almost doubled as well during the same period.

As a nation we now spend more than a *trillion dollars annually* on the media devices and media we consume. In fact, we consume so much media through so many different devices and channels that it's functionally impossible for anyone or any institution to know with any certainty just how much money our collective media habits cost us.

> **COLLECTIVELY, WE NOW SPEND MORE THAN A TRILLION DOLLARS ANNUALLY ON THE MEDIA DEVICES AND MEDIA WE CONSUME.**

Of course, with any other narcotic we typically only pay for what we consume. Not so with media, however. So intense is our media addiction that – so far at least – we are willing to pay most of our monthly cable, phone, and ISP bills with little or no regard for actual usage. Apparently, not only are we willing to pay for the media that we consume, but we're also willing to pay for the media that we *don't* consume – presumably so we can guarantee easy access to it when we need our next fix. I submit that the mere act of paying for a narcotic that we *don't* consume would likely fail to satisfy anyone's definition of sobriety, regardless of the narcotic and regardless of how they define addiction.

Indeed, if we diagnose addiction as the measure of excessive time and money we invest in our favorite drug(s), then the diagnosis of what's on the table in front of us in the

Great Age of Mediation is as crystal clear as our HDTV screens: *We are addicted – as individuals and as a culture – to media.*

WE ARE ADDICTED AS INDIVIDUALS *AND* AS A CULTURE TO MEDIA.

Not convinced? Ask yourself: "Could I devote the same time and money to any other behavior and somehow avoid the word addict to describe myself?" Or perhaps you simply don't believe the consumption numbers in the *Middletown Media Studies* report. Okay, cut the numbers in half, and then ask yourself the same question. No matter how we slice it, we invest more time and more money in media consumption than we invest in any other discretionary activity in our lives – including sleep – by far.

Of course no one puts a gun to our heads and forces us to watch TV or surf the Internet against our will. Media addiction, like all other addictions, is purely a demand-side problem. Again: *If it looks like a duck...*

WE INVEST MORE TIME IN MEDIA CONSUMPTION THAN WE INVEST IN ANY OTHER ACTIVITY, INCLUDING SLEEP.

Several thousand years ago the ancient Vedic Seers observed that we become our attention over time. They observed that we have a tendency to assume the characteristics of those things to which we devote our time and attention.

Thus, if we spend more time with God, they reasoned, we become more God-like. As we think in our hearts and minds, so we will become...

WE BECOME OUR ATTENTION.

Let's turn our attention now to the *Media Log*, a simple experiment designed to determine how much time and attention we devote to the media in our lives. The *Media Log* is based on two simple assertions, namely: that we can't deal with something that we can't see or fail to examine in the first place, and that a good measure of our daily media consumption is *unconscious.*

The *Media* Log renders the invisible visible and helps us understand exactly how we become our attention. It was designed to raise our awareness, to make us conscious of how and where and with whom we engage the media, particularly electronic media, and thereby how and where and with whom we spend our time.

So take a look at and feel free to copy the form on the next page.

Media Log		
Time	Medium	Foreground/Background

As you can see from the form, the *Media Log* exercise itself is the essence of simplicity: All you do is jot down every encounter with media throughout one typical weekday. Electronic media include the usual suspects: TV, video games, radio, the Internet, email, iPods and other portable music devices, mobile phones, and personal information managers (PIMs). Print media include newspapers, magazines, pamphlets, books, and billboards.

For each encounter, record the time of the encounter, the specific medium, and the nature of the encounter: *foreground* or *background.* A foreground encounter is one where you actively engage the medium in the foreground of your consciousness. For instance, listening to the news on the radio, talking on the phone, watching TV, checking your email and reading a book or a billboard all qualify as active engagements with the media, and likewise qualify as foreground encounters.

FOREGROUND MEDIA ARE THOSE YOU ACTIVELY AND CONSCIOUSLY ENGAGE.

By contrast, a background encounter is one in which you become aware of the medium but don't directly engage it. Background media are ambient; they blend into the background. You may notice them, but you choose not to actively engage them. Hence, you may notice billboards or graffiti along the highway, but if you don't read them, they qualify only as background encounters. Likewise, you may notice elevator music but not actually listen to it. You may notice the glare of a TV in a darkened room, but decide – for whatever reason – not to watch it.

> **BACKGROUND MEDIA ARE AMBIENT;**
> **THEY BLEND INTO THE BACKGROUND.**
> **YOU MAY NOTICE THEM, BUT YOU DON'T**
> **ENGAGE THEM.**

Since the Media Log exercise is all about awareness (and not memory), it's better to record each encounter as it occurs – as you become aware of it – rather than rely on your ability to recall it later. Don't be surprised, however, if you're worksheet fills up pretty quickly, and don't be surprised if the exercise becomes more and more demanding as the day wears on.

In fact, don't be surprised if you don't make it through an entire day with the *Media Log.* Most people simply don't; I didn't either on my first few attempts. We quit in part because we discover that there are simply too many encounters with media in our lives to record, in part because we frequently encounter or engage multiple media at the same time, and in part because introduction of the *Media Log* exercise itself adds yet another level of engagement and complexity to an already difficult and demanding daily schedule.

Later, when you get the chance, steal a few quiet moments to review the entries in your *Media Log.* You may notice some interesting patterns. For instance, you may notice that the number of background encounters increases disproportionately with the number of recorded entries – likely a result of the suddenly heightened media awareness imposed by the *Media Log* exercise itself; the mere act of observing your own behavior heightens your self awareness. You may also notice that a large percentage of your total media encounters are aural; they engage you through your ears. (Typically, the media we hear are more emotive – often more irritating or otherwise evocative – than those we just see.) Or you may notice just how frequently you consume print and electronic media at the same time; usually, the print is the foreground encounter, while the electronic media assumes an ambient background role. You may also notice that your foreground encounters with print are far more demanding than your foreground encounters with their electronic counterparts, although the electronic media are *far* more compelling, evocative, and addictive.

THE NUMBER OF BACKGROUND MEDIA ENCOUNTERS SEEMS TO INCREASE WITH AWARENESS.

THE MEDIA WE HEAR ARE MORE EVOCATIVE THAN THOSE WE SEE.

PRINT IS MORE DEMANDING, BUT ELECTRONIC MEDIA ARE FAR MORE COMPELLING, EVOCATIVE, AND ADDICTIVE.

Of course the primary revelation that emerges from the *Media Log* exercise by now will come as no surprise to you: *Our lives are totally and irrefutably immersed in media.*

WE ARE UTTERLY IMMERSED IN MEDIA.

Likewise it should come as no surprise that our addiction to the media comes at a price. Every addiction does. All technologies and all addictions – media not least – are Faustian bargains. They all come with a price tag. In the prescient words of the late great media ecologist Neil Postman:

> "*The invention of the printing press is an excellent example. Printing fostered the modern idea of individuality but it destroyed the medieval sense of community and social integration. Printing created prose but made poetry into an exotic and elitist form of expression. Printing made modern science possible but transformed religious sensibility into an exercise in superstition. Printing assisted in the growth of the nation-state but, in so doing, made patriotism into a sordid if not a murderous emotion.*
>
> "*Another way of saying this is that a new technology tends to favor some groups of people and harms other groups. School teachers, for example, will, in the long run, probably be made obsolete by television, as blacksmiths were made obsolete by the automobile, as balladeers were made obsolete by the printing press. Technolog-*

ical change, in other words, always results in winners and losers."

ALL TECHNOLOGIES AND ALL ADDICTIONS ARE FAUSTIAN BARGAINS. THEY ALL COME WITH A PRICE TAG.

Yes, all technologies come with hooks attached. There are no free rides, just as no good deeds go unpunished. Although schooled in a yeshiva, a Jewish parochial school, Mr. Postman himself was not a particularly religious man. He was, however, a protégé of the great Catholic prophet and media ecologist Marshall McLuhan, whose brilliant observation that *the medium is the message* rightfully constitutes the cornerstone of all media literacy and media ecology studies worldwide. But if the medium is indeed the message, what happens to the message when we, dear reader, become addicted to the medium? What if we wake up one morning to find ourselves suddenly on the painful losing end of our relationship with the media? What if we're already there? Where will we turn for help, and how much will it cost us to fix the problem? What's the price tag, and how do we pay for our addiction to the media?

IF THE MEDIUM IS THE MESSAGE, WHAT HAPPENS TO THE MESSAGE WHEN WE BECOME ADDICTED TO THE MEDIUM?

A few more questions to ponder for now: Where do we see room for God in our respective *Media Logs?* If almost all of our waking time is devoted to media consumption, what's left over for God? What happens to the quality of our lives when we *choose* to put God last?

> **WHERE IS THE TIME FOR GOD IN OUR LIVES, AND WHAT HAPPENS WHEN WE PUT GOD LAST?**

Chapter 4 Summary

ADDICTION IS ALMOST ALWAYS
DIAGNOSED AS A MEASURE OF HOW
MUCH TIME AND MONEY THE ADDICT
DEVOTES TO HIS OR HER FAVORITE
DRUG(S).

ADDICTION IS NEVER ABOUT THE
SPECIFIC DRUG. RATHER, IT'S ABOUT
BEHAVIOR. IT'S ABOUT HOW WE SPEND
OUR TIME AND MONEY.

THE AVERAGE AMERICAN ADULT
CONSUMES 11.7 HOURS OF MEDIA
EACH AND EVERY DAY.

COLLECTIVELY, WE NOW SPEND MORE
THAN A TRILLION DOLLARS ANNUALLY
ON THE MEDIA DEVICES AND MEDIA WE
CONSUME.

WE ARE ADDICTED AS INDIVIDUALS *AND*
AS A CULTURE TO MEDIA.

WE INVEST MORE TIME IN MEDIA
CONSUMPTION THAN WE INVEST IN ANY
OTHER ACTIVITY, INCLUDING SLEEP.

WE BECOME OUR ATTENTION.

FOREGROUND MEDIA ARE THOSE YOU
ACTIVELY AND CONSCIOUSLY ENGAGE.

Chapter 4 Summary (cont'd)

BACKGROUND MEDIA ARE AMBIENT;
THEY BLEND INTO THE BACKGROUND.
YOU MAY NOTICE THEM, BUT YOU DON'T
ENGAGE THEM.

THE NUMBER OF BACKGROUND MEDIA
ENCOUNTERS SEEMS TO INCREASE
WITH AWARENESS.

THE MEDIA WE HEAR ARE MORE
EVOCATIVE THAN THOSE WE SEE.

PRINT IS MORE DEMANDING, BUT
ELECTRONIC MEDIA ARE FAR MORE
COMPELLING, EVOCATIVE, AND
ADDICTIVE.

WE ARE UTTERLY IMMERSED IN MEDIA.

ALL TECHNOLOGIES AND ALL
ADDICTIONS ARE FAUSTIAN BARGAINS.
THEY ALL COME WITH A PRICE TAG.

IF THE MEDIUM IS THE MESSAGE, WHAT
HAPPENS TO THE MESSAGE WHEN WE
BECOME ADDICTED TO THE MEDIUM?

WHERE IS THE TIME FOR GOD IN OUR
LIVES, AND WHAT HAPPENS WHEN WE
PUT GOD LAST?

My Notes

My Notes

Chapter 5
And quacks like a duck...

Dear God,

Help me be vigilant. Give me strength and wisdom. Help me put you first in my life. Give me patience and fortitude. Help me better appreciate the good things in my life, those things that unfold slowly and reveal their beauty and grace like summer wildflowers. Help me resist those things that would accelerate my life, steal my freedom, and leave me empty. Help me instead to take the time to smell the roses, Lord. Help me take the time to listen, to hear your word and do your will. Amen.

Many who have performed The *Media Log* exercise tell me afterwards that they are simply appalled by their own seemingly endless appetite for all things media. They find themselves dismayed and disappointed by their own suddenly revealed capacity for excess. They feel betrayed, angered and ashamed by their own human weakness and vulnerability, and victimized by their own environments – *exactly* how addicts feel.

In response, some have admitted to pulling the plugs right away on all of their TVs and assorted electronic gadgets. That response, however, misses the point, and – like most New Year's resolutions – usually doesn't remain in effect for very long in any event. True, extreme responses sometimes help us feel better (or at least more righteous) initially, but they rarely get us where we want to be in the end, and sometimes do more harm than good.

Admittedly, the *Media Log* was conceived for its shock value. It was designed specifically to disrupt the unconscious patterns of our behavior and jar our sensibilities in the hope that our capacity for excess would be suddenly and rudely exposed in the process. It works pretty well that way, but the point of the exercise is not to provoke an extreme response. The objective of this book is not to replace one form of extreme behavior with another; rather, the ultimate behavioral objective of *Put God First* is to engender *moderation* instead. And we have a long ways to go before we can get from here to there. The *Media Log* is but one tiny step in the right direction, just as waking up in the morning is but the overture to a new day. So don't be impatient, because impatience – especially in the *Great Age of Mediation* – is high on the list of our own worst enemies.

All of the above, however, must be tempered by the sober understanding that we don't start out as addicts in life, just as no one aspires to become one. Addiction, like excess, creeps up on us. We typically ignore its steady encroachment in our lives until something adverse happens, unless or until we somehow bottom out: Maybe a relationship falls apart under the strain. Maybe we lose a job. Maybe our health fails. Or maybe bankruptcy dangles over our heads like the proverbial Sword of Damocles. I speak from personal experience with all of the above. None of it, however, just happened to me. As with everything else in life, my own complicity conspired with circumstance over time. I know from personal experience that God's ways are not my ways. I know also from personal experience that we *choose* to act out our addictions just as we *choose* also to ignore the consequences.

> ## WE TYPICALLY IGNORE ADDICTION IN OUR LIVES UNTIL WE SOMEHOW BOTTOM OUT.

Yet how did we arrive at a time when we suddenly know more about the cult of Hollywood than we know about our own family histories? How did we reach the point where we spend more time in front of the TV every day than we do with our kids? At what point did our healthcare system become the landfill for all of our media-induced physical and emotional excess? When did endless entertainment become the focal point of our lives? How and when did such massive excess enter our lives and assume center stage? When did we decide to put God dead last in the hierarchy of things that consume our time and attention?

For many of us, all of the above just seemed to happen – like the addiction that ensued. It all snuck up on us. We opened our eyes one day and there we were, suddenly awash in the detritus of our own excess, and bored to tears, in spite of our personal access to thousands of TV and radio channels, tens of millions of websites, weblogs and podcasts, and thousands of downloaded songs – each and every one designed specifically to rivet our attention and keep us occupied, at least for the next few seconds. But again, addiction is cunning that way; it almost always takes us by surprise…

**ADDICTION IS CUNNING.
IT SNEAKS UP ON US.**

Can you remember a time in your life – prior to the mid-1990s, prior to the introduction of the Internet and the explosion of digital productivity tools that sped unimpeded through the digital pipeline from our offices into our homes – when media were not as rapacious or all-consuming in our lives? Can you remember how much simpler and civil life was before we blurred the once cardinal distinction between home and office? Can you remember what it was like before we bargained away our leisure time for the largely mythic lure of unimagined wealth and early retirement during the heady dot com days? Can you remember a time when pedophiles didn't seem to threaten our children on every street corner? Can you remember a time when children played *unattended* on that same street corner? Can you remember a time when you could phone a company and talk to a real human being, when companies that profess excellent customer service weren't hermetically sealed off from their customers by voicemail and email? Can you remember a time when you didn't shop for doctors by zip code?

Of course we can't turn back the clock, and the past in reality was never as rosy or Utopian as it sometimes seems in retrospect. There's also something to be said for some sort of emotional safe harbor to protect and free us from our own histories. Indeed, that's what America is all about; America is where people come to escape the tyranny of their own histories. After all, America was founded by *dissident* Protestants who sailed thousands of miles just to flee their own European history of religious oppression.

As a result, history is almost anathema to American culture, especially American pop culture. The freedom that the Founding Fathers codified and introduced to the world stage back in the 18th century was simply extraordinary in the confluence of historically unique events and circumstances that produced it, and nothing remotely like it had been witnessed since Moses parted the Red Sea and marched the Israelites out of Egypt, *away* from their own history and towards a new destiny. But the saga didn't end for Moses and the Israelites when they escaped Pharaoh. No, that was just the beginning; they spent the next forty years wandering the Sinai while they effectively *purged* their history as slaves and idol worshipers – all in anticipation of and preparation for the *redemption* they would find in their new home, the Promised

Land. American freedom, like the freedom entrusted by God to the ancient Hebrews, is freedom from our own pasts – and likewise offers a solemn promise of redemption. And while our addiction to media certainly helps us flee and purge our own histories (and everything else), it offers a false freedom and redemption in exchange. In fact, it doesn't free us at all; it imprisons us instead. And it doesn't redeem us; it ransoms our freedom for expedience, cheap thrills, and empty promises.

The sudden and massive introduction of digital bandwidth in the mid-1990s imposed immediate and enormous changes on our lives, not least of which was a tsunami of commercial media that rushed in to fill an ever-widening digital pipeline – not to mention almost every waking moment of our lives. Not once, however, did we stop to question our own behavior (something not peculiar to Americans, and something we seldom if ever do in any era). Not once did we pause to examine what might happen to us in transition from the analog to the digital age, or how that transition might translate into and affect our lifestyles for better or worse. We were far too busy building digital kingdoms, slaying analog dragons, and sipping designer vodkas to notice or care. We were utterly entertained, utterly complicit in, and utterly oblivious to our own excessive behavior. Please take note: Entertainment and oblivious complicity are the simple ingredients for addiction in the *Great Age of Mediation*. *If it quacks like a duck...*

> **WE ARE LARGELY COMPLICIT IN AND
> OBLIVIOUS TO OUR OWN EXCESSIVE
> BEHAVIOR.**

The sudden explosion of media in the mid-1990s was fueled by hundreds of billions of dollars of investment capital, all of it powered by a billion microchips. Together, promiscuous money and unbridled technology ushered in The *Great Age of Mediation*. We partied for the next five years in what can only be described as a stupefying addictive binge. Then we crashed. And when we awoke the next morning we discovered that our dreams, our money, and our time were all long gone – survived only by our digital devices and our addictions to them. Like all good addicts, however, we started planning for the next party right away. But the dot com promises of endless prosperity and youthful retirement had skipped town, and taken with them many of our dreams and aspirations. In the wake of their speedy exodus they left behind only fear and envy, the true legacies of all addiction.

> **THE DOT COM ERA OF THE LATE 1990S
> WAS NOTHING LESS THAN A
> STUPEFYING ADDICTIVE BINGE.**

I remember when I lost my job in 2001, not long after the dot com economy crashed and burned. As a confirmed workaholic who rarely spent fewer than 65 hours per week in the office, it never once occurred to yours truly not to take

69

all of my office productivity tools – my laptop, my PDA, and my cell phone – home with me that final day, despite the fact that I suddenly had no work to do, no meetings to schedule, and no phone calls to make. But I discovered not long afterwards that the presence of so much gratuitous digital technology in my life was kind of like riding a stationary bike: I was going nowhere fast, fully equipped with a speedometer to tell me precisely how fast I wasn't going, and an odometer to tell me exactly how far I hadn't gone. The time I had once filled with work I now filled trying to find or manufacture work. But my digital gadgets, and my obsessions with them, didn't change at all. Apparently, party planning was never my strong suit...

As mentioned in Chapter 4, addiction is never about the specific drug. Rather, addiction is about behavior. And the mechanics of addiction are always pretty much the same, irrespective of the drug. In a nutshell, addiction rewires our brains over time as we repeat the same compulsive behaviors again and again. It usurps and coops all of our inborn self-protection and self-preservation mechanisms in the process, then puts them to work instead on its own behalf. That's why it's possible for us as addicts to consistently choose behaviors that we *know* run contrary to our own better interests, behaviors that we *know* might result in dire consequences. That's why we insist on that last drink at the bar before we jump in the car to drive home. That's why we place that final bet at the track before running to the bank to cover our losses. That's why we watch that final half hour of late-night television instead of getting some much needed sleep. That's why we insist on surfing the Web instead of playing with our kids. We *choose* to do all of these things despite the fact that we *know* better.

Moderating character attributes like common sense, reason, personal ethics, and faith – attributes that ordinarily protect us and promote our welfare – are routinely suppressed, dismissed, and overruled by the more primitive, immediate, and self-destructive demands of our addictions. Those relationships most attuned to excess rise in the hierarchies of our rewired minds while those that champion moderation – including and especially our relationship with God – whither in the exchange.

ADDICTION REWIRES OUR BRAINS, AND USURPS OUR INBORN SELF-PROTECTION AND SELF-PRESERVATION MECHANISMS.

All of our thoughts and aspirations are passed first through the lens of our media addiction, where they are thoroughly assessed and filtered. Those things that promote moderation – like personal values and our relationship with God – are filtered out or modified en route. Those things that promote excess in the interest of the addiction are assigned to the fast track.

ALL OF OUR THOUGHTS AND ASPIRATIONS ARE PASSED FIRST THROUGH THE LENS OF OUR MEDIA ADDICTION.

71

Thus do our addictions set themselves up as our emotional and intellectual gatekeepers, as the moderators and arbiters of all of our internal debates – the *identical* function assumed in recent years by the explosion of commercial media in our lives. As the primary gatekeeper to and moderator over all of our internal debates, our addiction to media promotes excess and promiscuity in virtually all things, media consumption first and foremost. After all, no one ever got rich by selling *less* of anything, and contrary to popular belief, the ads aren't there to support the programs; the programs are there to support the ads. Contrary to what our addictions may whisper sweetly in our ears, they're not here to support us; we're here to support them.

OUR ADDICTIONS SET THEMSELVES UP AS OUR EMOTIONAL AND INTELLECTUAL GATEKEEPERS, AS THE MODERATORS AND ARBITERS OF ALL OUR INTERNAL DEBATES. JUST LIKE THE MEDIA.

OUR ADDICTION TO MEDIA PROMOTES EXCESS AND PROMISCUITY IN ALL THINGS, MEDIA CONSUMPTION FIRST AND FOREMOST.

We've all heard ourselves and others claim addiction to specific TV or radio programs. Some folks claim addictions to soap operas, and some are self-professed news junkies. But again, addiction isn't about the specific narcotic. We don't crave the programs; we crave the *feelings* – the pleasure and relief – they so reliably invoke. Proof that addiction is not about the specific drug resides in the simple observation that we don't consume less media when our favorite programs get cancelled any more than a heroin addict consumes less heroin when his favorite neighborhood dealer gets pinched. We just find new programs and new dealers to satisfy our habits instead.

> ## WE DON'T CRAVE THE PROGRAMS; WE CRAVE THE FEELINGS THEY INVOKE.

In the *Great Age of Mediation*, the media are no longer at our disposal; rather, we are at the media's disposal. For all of the talk about empowered consumers, commercial advertisers *target* us far more frequently and aggressively than they seek our permission, and greater choice does not necessarily translate into greater freedom. In the *Great Age of Mediation* we have far more channels but far less diversity of thought. We have more opinions but less time to consider them. In the end, our addiction to the media – like all addictions – resembles a benevolent despot: It provides comfort and succor and false security in exchange for our utter fealty. But even the most benevolent despots are still despots. They don't work for us; we work for them.

**EVEN THE MOST BENEVOLENT DESPOTS
ARE STILL DESPOTS. OUR ADDICTIONS
DON'T WORK FOR US;
WE WORK FOR THEM.**

In theory, the media give us the technological where-withal to reach out like never before. In practice, however, our addiction to the media *isolates* us (just consult your *Media Log* to see how frequently you consume media alone), and we become more risk averse as our media consumption habits become increasingly personalized.

**OUR ADDICTION TO MEDIA ISOLATES US,
AND WE BECOME MORE RISK AVERSE
AS OUR MEDIA CONSUMPTION HABITS
BECOME INCREASINGLY
PERSONALIZED.**

While we have the technological ability to network with and engage more and more people, we typically circum-scribe our personal networks to and spend time with those who already share our interests and passions. We wind up perpetually preaching to our own choirs, hermetically sealed off from and wary of any thoughts or passions that don't precisely coincide with our own – despite the fact that our "personal" networks continue to expand exponentially.

The same basic social phenomenon occurs with addicts: They engage with and confine themselves to those who share the same addiction. Opium dens, crack houses, bars, adult emporiums, and digital social networks and communities are each full of addicts who all share the same addictions and self-serving ritual behaviors. Indeed, the expressed intent of each acting-out venue – real or virtual – is to facilitate the addiction and provide safe harbor for addicts by confining them to their own company and isolating them from outside intervention.

In the *Great Age of Mediation*, however, our obsessions and addictions eventually turn against us; they seal us off from the rest of the world, despite the technological promise of a global village. At a certain point in the escalation of our addiction to media, our vastly accelerated technological ability to inspire and accrue virtual relationships simply *overwhelms* us. That's when we begin to deploy the very same communications tools that we use to build our virtual networks in a different capacity altogether; we suddenly rely on them to effectively *shut down* communications instead. This is why it's almost impossible nowadays to speak with a human being at a large corporation. They are *massively* overwhelmed and overmatched by their own sudden ability to engender *millions* of relationships – all of which have the equally sudden ability to talk back. So they deploy their communications technologies to effectively shut down communications and protect themselves from the sudden onslaught of consumers with questions, gripes, and suggestions. They use their communications technologies to hermetically seal themselves off from the rest of the world.

Like our corporate culture counterparts, each of us as individuals is compelled to spend more and more time deciding who we *don't* want to have relationships with, more and more time fending off the unsolicited entreaties of the thousands of *strangers* who now have access to the most intimate details of our lives. In short, we can reach out to more addicts, but we retreat more into ourselves and away from God in the process. This retreat into ourselves is very much a typical function of addiction, of unrestrained behaviors suddenly coming home to roost. Again: *If it quacks like a duck...*

In fact, our lives are so crowded by media nowadays that there's barely room for God or anything else at all. Bit by bit, the self-serving rituals we build to sustain and promote our addiction to media replace the more meaningful rituals in our lives and thus erode the quality of our lives over time. The dinner table eventually gives way to the evening news while the evening news eventually gives way to celebrity worship and idolatry. Family picnics in the park on Sunday give way to all-day football coverage replete with all-day eating and drinking binges. The sounds of songbirds in the backyard give way to the sounds of TV in the background. Intimate family discussions give way to a cascade of cryptic instant messages and text messages, communiqués whose real intent – like email and voicemail – is to warn us away instead of welcome us in, to avoid communication, defer intimacy, and offer the *illusion* of accountability. Values give way to expedience and are replaced over time by a pervasive sense of *entitlement,* another standard feature of addiction; as addicts, we always believe ourselves *entitled* to our next fix.

**BIT BY BIT, THE SELF-SERVING RITUALS
WE BUILD TO PROMOTE AND SUSTAIN
OUR ADDICTION TO MEDIA REPLACE THE
MORE MEANINGFUL RITUALS IN OUR
LIVES AND THUS ERODE THE QUALITY OF
OUR LIVES.**

In the grips of our addiction to media, our lives and communities begin to mirror the commercial media landscape that shapes them: We become more narcissistic and less civil, more fragmented and less cohesive, more polarized and less patient with those who disagree, more mired in our own inertia and less inclined to innovate. We insist on more regulation to protect us and our communities against our own excessive behaviors, and surrender our freedoms in the process. Indeed, freedom is among the very first casualties of all addiction. As we exchange the responsibilities of freedom for the comforts and convenience of fealty, we become less attuned to and less capable of *prevention* and more predisposed to and invested in *post facto intervention*. We become less attached to the sacred and more invested in the profane.

**FREEDOM IS AMONG THE VERY FIRST
CASUALTIES OF ALL ADDICTION.**

Our unrestrained digital excess ultimately forsakes and betrays all sense of proportion and balance, and our vision is both circumscribed by and confined to the size of the screens

77

in front of us. We turn away from and reject the prophets of moderation and restraint while we surrender ourselves to a wildly seductive but suicidal electronic saturnalia. We are already – per the prescient title of Neil Postman's wonderful little book – deeply and almost irreversibly engaged in the process of *Amusing Ourselves to Death.*

> **WE ARE ENGAGED IN THE PROCESS OF**
> ***AMUSING OURSELVES TO DEATH.***

The Roman historian Livy (59 B.C. –A.D. 17) was less glib and a good deal more direct than Mr. Postman when he wrote about the rise of decadence throughout the empire: "Of late years wealth has made us greedy, and self-indulgence has brought us, through every form of sensual excess, to be, if I may so put it, in love with death both individual and collective." One can only wonder what Livy would have to say about the *Great Age of Mediation* two millennia later.

Over the years my theories about media as addiction and about addiction as a default condition of 21st-century America have been most severely criticized – not so surprisingly – by people in the media profession, including not only those who produce, buy and sell commercial media, but by those academicians and pedagogues who research media and teach media-related studies in schools and universities as well. For the most part, those engaged in the production and sale of media don't think very highly of those who – ensconced in ivory towers – research and teach media, and those who research and teach media largely distrust and distance themselves from those who – ensconced in corporate board rooms – produce, buy and sell media.

Of course, neither constituency has much use for yours truly, in part because no one wants to be called an addict, however apropos, and in part because I typically describe those of us who work in or with media as the *biggest* addicts. What both sides share, however, is an abiding willingness to dismiss the power of the media drugs that we collectively produce, buy, sell, research and teach, and an even greater blind faith in the power of our own intellects to somehow inure us against the narcotic effects of the drug that we immerse ourselves in throughout almost every waking hour of every single day. Stated otherwise, ours is simply the same old tried-and-true formula for addiction revisited: We dismiss the power of the narcotic while we profess the power to resist it.

> **OUR TRIED-AND-TRUE FORMULA FOR ADDICTION: WE DISMISS THE POWER OF THE NARCOTIC WHILE WE PROFESS THE STRENGTH TO RESIST IT.**

But intellect and reason are historically poor hedges against addiction, and offer even less protection against our addiction to media. In fact, intellect and reason are among addiction's primary tools to enforce its demands and strengthen its grip on us. The smarter we are, the easier it is for us to rationalize our own self-destructive and anti-social behavior. Thus, the media professionals – those of us who produce, buy, sell, research and teach media – may be the (self-professed) smartest rats in the maze, but we're still stuck in the same maze no matter how many times we find the cheese first.

INTELLECT AND REASON ARE HISTORICALLY POOR HEDGES AGAINST ADDICTION.

The mere fact that those of us who produce, distribute, buy, sell, and teach media are also the biggest media addicts distinguishes media addiction from all others. After all, no pharmaceutical company or foreign drug cartel could survive for long if those who produced, distributed, and sold the drugs were addicted to them. Likewise, any casino whose workers are all compulsive gamblers will crumble in a heartbeat. Of all the addictions, only media addiction so reliably imprisons the souls of those who produce, distribute, and sell the narcotic.

THE FACT THAT THOSE OF US WHO PRODUCE, DISTRIBUTE, BUY, SELL, AND TEACH MEDIA ARE THE BIGGEST MEDIA ADDICTS DISTINGUISHES MEDIA ADDICTION FROM ALL OTHERS.

Moreover, the mere fact that those of us who produce, distribute, buy, sell, research and teach media are the biggest media addicts is everywhere manifest in the narcotic itself;

the medium is very much the message – just one of the reasons why faith in God and religion are almost always portrayed in modern secular media as the havens of fanatics, lunatics, cultists, and the hopelessly naïve among us. But what some may interpret as a battle of religious superstition against enlightened reason is in fact our addiction's self-defense mechanism at work. Our addiction to media rightfully interprets God as a threat to its own power. But that's because the first function of all addiction is to drive out any competing gods and undermine or sabotage any moderating force that might otherwise challenge its hegemony.

The first objective of all addiction, therefore, is to weaken the moral and ethical fiber of the host in preparation for what will follow: a perpetual cycle of fear, distrust, envy, and shame – all of which combine not only to protect and promote the interests of the addiction itself, but to threaten the quality of our lives as well. And as we shall see in Chapter 6, fear, distrust, envy and shame are the primary weapons deployed by our addictions in their battles against God, and the collective reason why the quality of our lives is in decline in the *Great Age of Mediation*. We're simply too consumed with fear, distrust, envy and shame to focus on quality. Who's got the time?

> **OUR ADDICTION TO MEDIA RIGHTFULLY INTERPRETS GOD AS A THREAT TO ITS POWER.**

THE FIRST FUNCTION OF ALL ADDICTION
IS TO DRIVE OUT GOD.

FEAR, DISTRUST, ENVY AND SHAME ARE
THE PRIMARY WEAPONS DEPLOYED BY
OUR ADDICTIONS IN THEIR BATTLE
AGAINST GOD.

WE'RE SIMPLY TOO CONSUMED WITH
FEAR, DISTRUST, ENVY AND SHAME TO
FOCUS ON QUALITY.
WHO'S GOT THE TIME?

Chapter 5 Summary

WE TYPICALLY IGNORE ADDICTION IN OUR LIVES UNTIL WE SOMEHOW BOTTOM OUT.

ADDICTION IS CUNNING.
IT SNEAKS UP ON US.

WE ARE LARGELY COMPLICIT IN AND OBLIVIOUS TO OUR OWN EXCESSIVE BEHAVIOR.

THE DOT COM ERA OF THE LATE 1990s WAS NOTHING LESS THAN A STUPEFYING ADDICTIVE BINGE.

ADDICTION REWIRES OUR BRAINS, AND USURPS OUR INBORN SELF-PROTECTION AND SELF-PRESERVATION MECHANISMS.

ALL OF OUR THOUGHTS AND ASPIRATIONS ARE PASSED FIRST THROUGH THE LENS OF OUR MEDIA ADDICTION.

OUR ADDICTIONS SET THEMSELVES UP AS OUR EMOTIONAL AND INTELLECTUAL GATEKEEPERS, AS THE MODERATORS AND ARBITERS OF ALL OUR INTERNAL DEBATES. JUST LIKE THE MEDIA.

Chapter 5 Summary (cont'd)

OUR ADDICTION TO MEDIA PROMOTES
EXCESS AND PROMISCUITY IN ALL
THINGS, MEDIA CONSUMPTION
FIRST AND FOREMOST.

WE DON'T CRAVE THE PROGRAMS;
WE CRAVE THE FEELINGS THEY INVOKE.

EVEN THE MOST BENEVOLENT DESPOTS
ARE STILL DESPOTS. OUR
ADDICTIONS DON'T WORK FOR US;
WE WORK FOR THEM.

OUR ADDICTION TO MEDIA ISOLATES US,
AND WE BECOME MORE RISK AVERSE
AS OUR MEDIA CONSUMPTION HABITS
BECOME INCREASINGLY
PERSONALIZED.

BIT BY BIT, THE SELF-SERVING RITUALS
WE BUILD TO PROMOTE AND SUSTAIN
OUR ADDICTION TO MEDIA REPLACE THE
MORE MEANINGFUL RITUALS IN OUR
LIVES AND THUS ERODE THE QUALITY OF
OUR LIVES.

FREEDOM IS AMONG THE VERY FIRST
CASUALTIES OF ALL ADDICTION.

WE ARE ENGAGED IN THE PROCESS OF
AMUSING OURSELVES TO DEATH.

Chapter 5 Summary (cont'd)

OUR TRIED-AND-TRUE FORMULA FOR ADDICTION: WE DISMISS THE POWER OF THE NARCOTIC WHILE WE PROFESS THE STRENGTH TO RESIST IT.

INTELLECT AND REASON ARE HISTORICALLY POOR HEDGES AGAINST ADDICTION.

THE FACT THAT THOSE OF US WHO PRODUCE, DISTRIBUTE, BUY, SELL, AND TEACH MEDIA ARE THE BIGGEST MEDIA ADDICTS DISTINGUISHES MEDIA ADDICTION FROM ALL OTHERS.

OUR ADDICTION TO MEDIA RIGHTFULLY INTERPRETS GOD AS A THREAT TO ITS POWER.

THE FIRST FUNCTION OF ALL ADDICTION IS TO DRIVE OUT GOD.

FEAR, DISTRUST, ENVY AND SHAME ARE THE PRIMARY WEAPONS DEPLOYED BY OUR ADDICTIONS IN THEIR BATTLE AGAINST GOD.

WE'RE SIMPLY TOO CONSUMED WITH FEAR, DISTRUST, ENVY AND SHAME TO FOCUS ON QUALITY.
WHO'S GOT THE TIME?

My Notes

My Notes

Chapter 6
Stinking thinking...

Dear God,

I praise and adore you. Show me your favor, and teach me to expect good things. Show me your love and forgive my many weaknesses. I surrender all of my fear, all of my envy, and all of my shame to you. Take them from me, and walk with me in victory. Help me be grateful to you always – for I am nothing without you, drowning in a sea of your abundance. Amen.

Where's God in our lives? We cannot set Him aside and somehow expect to appreciate His abundance. We cannot worship others before Him and somehow anticipate His favor. We cannot forsake Him without forsaking ourselves in the process.

Through our addiction to media we have fashioned for ourselves a near Godless environment, one in which virtually every waking moment is filled with addiction-induced fear, distrust, envy, and shame. All of the formerly moderating influences and institutions in our lives – family, community, and religion – are now under sustained and crippling attack by a *massive* addiction whose only imperative is pure *carpe diem,* unfettered consumption of and entitlement to everything right now, especially more media. Those attributes – faith in God, hard work, deferred gratification, humility, patriotism, and personal sacrifice – that we once viewed as vital contributors to the quality of our lives, our communities, and our country, we now view as hopelessly naïve, irrelevant, and passé. But we hardly notice their absence, in part because there can be no profanity among men when *everything* is profane, and in part because we have set no time aside to consider or mourn our loss. In the *Great Age of Mediation*, we have reserved no room at the inn for God.

FAITH IN GOD, HARD WORK, DEFERRED GRATIFICATION, HUMILITY, PATRIOTISM, AND PERSONAL SACRIFICE ARE NOW CONSIDERED HOPELESSLY NAÏVE, IRRELEVANT, AND PASSÉ.

THERE CAN BE NO PROFANITY AMONG MEN WHEN EVERYTHING IS PROFANE.

IN THE *GREAT AGE OF MEDIATION*, WE HAVE RESERVED NO ROOM AT THE INN FOR GOD.

Fear, distrust, envy and shame: such are the driving emotions and byproducts of all addiction, media addiction no less. One morning on a whim, I set aside a mere ten minutes to flip randomly through my cable TV channels and write down the various threats and dangers that the media considered important enough – for whatever reason – to share with me that morning. The following *Short List of Things to Fear and Distrust* emerged…

Short List of Things to Fear and Distrust	
▪ China	▪ terrorists
▪ neighbors	▪ open borders
▪ retirement	▪ closed borders
▪ incontinence	▪ religious fanatics
▪ rogue comets	▪ illicit drugs
▪ predatory teachers	▪ Democrats
▪ predatory clergy	▪ global warming
▪ identity theft	▪ boredom
▪ Republicans	▪ acid indigestion
▪ gum disease	▪ restless leg syndrome

Please bear in mind that the above *Short List of Things to Fear and Distrust* was compiled from a mere ten-minute exposure to cable television. Now remember that the average American consumes *11.7 hours* of media each and every day – or about *70 times* longer than it took me to compile my *Short List of Things to Fear and Distrust.* The numbers alone beg some questions: *What are we doing to ourselves?* How do we bring ourselves to even get out of bed in the morning in the relentless promise of so much fear? Or consider the opposite: How great and influential still is our vestigial faith, and why do we deny and dismiss it in spite of its obvious power to imbue in us our hopes and aspirations for a better future? Nowadays, the fact that we even get out of bed each morning in the face of so much abject fear testifies not to reason at all, but to *sheer faith.* It's nothing short of a modern miracle.

HOW CAN WE POSSIBLY DEAL WITH THE PROSPECT OF SO MUCH MEDIA-INDUCED FEAR?

HOW GREAT AND POWERFUL STILL IS OUR VESTIGIAL FAITH? AND WHY DO WE DENY AND DISMISS IT?

Still, our fears seem to multiply faster than our faith in the *Great Age of Mediation*. Enough is never enough – not nearly. We live our lives in constant fear of not enough money, not enough food, not enough prestige, not enough excitement, not enough security, not enough sex, not enough education, not enough information, not enough respect, not enough health, not enough peace of mind, and not nearly enough time to acquire all of the above.

In the *Great Age of Mediation*, we are taught to fear and distrust everything and everyone. It begins with the media-driven fear that a relationship with God will somehow compromise our ability to think clearly. In the vacuum once occupied by our explicit faith, we are taught instead to fear and distrust our neighbors, our teachers, our clergy, our leaders, our healers, our pasts and our futures. We are taught to fear and distrust anyone who takes a risk, anyone who offers in good faith and charity to lend a hand, even while we are extolled to invite massive excess into our lives.

IN THE *GREAT AGE OF MEDIATION*, ENOUGH IS NEVER ENOUGH.

Indeed, the driving technology behind all commercial media nowadays is the exact same technology that drives every corporation on the planet: the electronic spreadsheet. It's where we deposit all of our commercial dreams and aspirations *first,* and its primary functions – to project scale and mitigate risk – are identical irrespective of specific corporate charter. Thus the same electronic spreadsheet culture that drives FOX News drives NPR and PBS, just as the same spreadsheet culture that drives the giant pharmaceutical companies drives the Colombian drug cartels. Everyone wants more for less, and like all cultures, ours is driven by our tools. In the *Great Age of Mediation*, however, we become – like our tools – increasingly risk-averse as the scale they project and promote accelerates and escalates far beyond our ability to comprehend the consequences.

But risk aversion has an obvious downside: Who needs faith in the absence of risk? And how can we possibly mitigate the risk associated with such massive scale if *everyone* is inflating their numbers by default? For instance, there is almost no way to distinguish the website of a global conglomerate from the website of a mom and pop shop, as long as either mom or pop have the wherewithal to design and build a solid online presence. What we get in the end seems to reflect the essential conflict of scale versus risk that the sheer ubiquity and power of the electronic spreadsheet engenders. In the end, in the presence of almost unfathomable scale, there is precious little if any accountability to show for all of our aversion to risk. It seems to me that we pray for success while we set ourselves up for an inevitable per-pwalk.

WHO NEEDS FAITH IN THE ABSENCE OF RISK?

When we aren't consumed by fear and distrust in the *Great Age of Mediation*, we are consumed by envy and shame instead, the flip side of the same toxic coin. Envy is the gateway to self-serving ritual, and the shame that our self-serving rituals invoke in us only drives us deeper into ourselves. Together – as co-conspirators with fear and distrust – they constitute the perfect storm environment for addiction and excess to thrive.

We live our lives consumed with distrust and envy for those who already have the things we want but don't have, and driven or paralyzed by the fear that we will somehow come up short in our erstwhile efforts to attain them. Shame is what we feel whenever we pause long enough to come up for air. Shame breathes through the cracks in our busy days. Fear, envy and shame are all kissing cousins, all members of an incestuous relationship that breeds an illegitimate sense of bottomless deprivation. In the *Great Age of Mediation*, we distrust God and live our lives immersed in the perception of overwhelming deprivation while we drown in a sea of excess.

> **OUR LIVES ARE CONSUMED WITH FEAR,
> DISTRUST, ENVY AND SHAME.**

> **SHAME IS WHAT WE FEEL WHENEVER
> WE PAUSE LONG ENOUGH TO COME UP
> FOR AIR IN THE *GREAT AGE OF MEDIA-
> TION*.**

> **WE DISTRUST GOD AND LIVE OUR LIVES
> IMMERSED IN THE PERCEPTION OF
> OVERWHELMING DEPRIVATION WHILE
> WE DROWN IN A SEA OF EXCESS.**

Our addiction to media merely breeds more fear, more distrust, more envy, more shame, and more excess – including more media consumption. Before we know it, our lives are full of what recovering addicts call *stinking thinking*, the emotional backbone of all addiction and – not coincidentally – all commercial media.

> **OUR LIVES ARE CONSUMED WITH
> STINKING THINKING.**

According to our media addiction, the *only* possible remedy for or protection against all of the stinking thinking in our lives – all of the fear and distrust and envy – is the consumption of even more media. It's the exact same generic prescription offered by all addictions: All we ever really need is the very next fix.

Our addiction to media promises to provide solutions for any and every problem, especially boredom. Regardless of the problem, however, every solution offered up by our media addiction begins and ends with more media (stay tuned), just as each addictive cycle begins and ends with a barrage of stinking thinking.

> **EACH ADDICTIVE CYCLE BEGINS AND ENDS WITH STINKING THINKING.**

All of which leads us back to the question raised in Chapter 4: If the medium is the message, what happens to the message when we become addicted to the medium? The answer is found in the title of Chapter 3. The message in all addiction, regardless of the narcotic, is always the same: *Eat all you want, we'll make more.* Indeed, *more* is the *only* conceivable response to the impoverishment of stinking thinking in the *Great Age of Mediation*.

> **THE MESSAGE OF ALL ADDICTION IS ALWAYS THE SAME, REGARDLESS OF THE NARCOTIC: EAT ALL YOU WANT, WE'LL MAKE MORE.**

Our addiction to media promises everything, but can only deliver more of the same: more media, more sex, more credit, more gambling, more fast food, more prescription drugs, more liquor, more tobacco, and more stinking thinking. In the *Great Age of Mediation*, we have all but eliminated God and handed the entire War Against Drugs over to the biggest dealers on the block.

> **OUR ADDICTIONS PROMISE THE WORLD,**
> **BUT CAN ONLY DELIVER**
> **MORE ADDICTION.**

> **IN THE *GREAT AGE OF MEDIATION*, WE**
> **HAVE ELIMINATED GOD, AND HANDED**
> **THE ENTIRE WAR AGAINST DRUGS**
> **OVER TO THE BIGGEST DEALERS**
> **ON THE BLOCK.**

Our media addiction – like all addictions – relies on our willingness to dismiss its power. It wants us to think that we are somehow in control of our habits, when the exact opposite is true: They control us. And while we are certainly *responsible* for them, we hardly *control* them, at least not if the value exchange – what we get in return for the time and money that we invest in them – is any indication. All indications in the *Great Age of Mediation* are that we consistently sell ourselves short; we sell ourselves cheap.

> **IN THE *GREAT AGE OF MEDIATION*,**
> **WE SELL OURSELVES SHORT,**
> **WE SELL OURSELVES CHEAP.**

And while it's certainly true – as some skeptics argue – that religion sells faith in God, our addiction to media sells *everything* else. And right now, our addiction to media is winning the sales battle, hands down.

Chapter 6 Summary

FAITH IN GOD, HARD WORK,
DEFERRED GRATIFICATION,
HUMILITY, PATRIOTISM, AND
PERSONAL SACRIFICE ARE NOW
CONSIDERED HOPELESSLY NAÏVE,
IRRELEVANT, AND PASSÉ.

THERE CAN BE NO PROFANITY AMONG
MEN WHEN EVERYTHING IS PROFANE.

IN THE *GREAT AGE OF MEDIATION*, WE
HAVE RESERVED NO ROOM AT THE INN
FOR GOD.

HOW CAN WE POSSIBLY DEAL WITH THE
PROSPECT OF SO MUCH
MEDIA-INDUCED FEAR?

HOW GREAT AND POWERFUL STILL IS
OUR VESTIGIAL FAITH? AND WHY DO
WE DENY AND DISMISS IT?

IN THE *GREAT AGE OF MEDIATION*,
ENOUGH IS NEVER ENOUGH.

WHO NEEDS FAITH IN THE
ABSENCE OF RISK?

OUR LIVES ARE CONSUMED WITH FEAR,
DISTRUST, ENVY AND SHAME.

Chapter 6 Summary (cont'd)

SHAME IS WHAT WE FEEL WHENEVER WE PAUSE LONG ENOUGH TO COME UP FOR AIR IN THE *GREAT AGE OF MEDIATION*.

WE DISTRUST GOD AND LIVE OUR LIVES IMMERSED IN THE PERCEPTION OF OVERWHELMING DEPRIVATION WHILE WE DROWN IN A SEA OF EXCESS.

OUR LIVES ARE CONSUMED WITH STINKING THINKING.

EACH ADDICTIVE CYCLE BEGINS AND ENDS WITH STINKING THINKING.

THE MESSAGE OF ALL ADDICTION IS ALWAYS THE SAME, REGARDLESS OF THE NARCOTIC: EAT ALL YOU WANT, WE'LL MAKE MORE.

OUR ADDICTIONS PROMISE THE WORLD, BUT CAN ONLY DELIVER MORE ADDICTION.

IN THE *GREAT AGE OF MEDIATION*, WE HAVE ELIMINATED GOD, AND HANDED THE ENTIRE WAR AGAINST DRUGS OVER TO THE BIGGEST DEALERS ON THE BLOCK.

IN THE *GREAT AGE OF MEDIATION*, WE SELL OURSELVES SHORT, WE SELL OURSELVES CHEAP.

My Notes

My Notes

Part III

The Quality of Life
Redeemed

Chapter 7
You can intervene on me...

Dear God,

Thank you for your loving guidance and patience. I surrender to you all of my defects of character, and pray you will forgive my trespasses. Please enter my life. Strengthen me where I am weak. Cleanse my heart and soul, and steel my resolve. Make me ready to receive your word and do your will. Amen.

What begins as a trickle ends in a flood, and we will be renewed by the transforming of our minds and spirits. Unfortunately, it's far too late to prevent endemic media addiction in 21st-century America; obsessive-compulsive behavior and addiction are *already* the default conditions. We *already* spend almost all of our waking time in the act of consuming media, and there are few if any indications that we have learned as a society how to moderate or otherwise regulate our insatiable appetite for all things media. Indeed, all of the media consumption statistics indicate the exact opposite, and all of the technologies designed to help us control or personalize our media consumption – including the remote control, the VCR, downloadable music and video, the DVR and video on demand – have so far only increased it.

Clearly, our addiction to media is still growing, and has yet to plateau. And while we probably shouldn't expect to see any *just say no to media* public service announcements on television anytime soon, we have already witnessed the first few of what will doubtless be many more consumer lawsuits against media franchises – like those already filed against the tobacco and fast food industries – as the fallout of our media addiction compounds over time.

IT'S FAR TOO LATE TO PREVENT MEDIA ADDICTION IN AMERICA.

And while it may be too late to prevent media addiction in the *Great Age of Mediation*, we can however make the choice to change our behavior and improve the quality of life for ourselves and our families *today!* In fact, this little book in your hands indicates that you have already decided to make that choice. By doing so, you pronounce your faith in God as well. Please know that you won't be alone in your journey, for He has already promised to help those who have faith in Him.

> **WE CAN MAKE THE CHOICE TO IMPROVE THE QUALITY OF LIFE FOR OURSELVES AND OUR FAMILIES *TODAY!***

> **GOD WILL HELP THOSE WHO HAVE FAITH IN HIM.**

As some of you doubtless already know, most mainstream addiction recovery programs in this country, including almost all 12-step programs, stress abstinence as the key to recovery. But what you may not know – and doubtless won't learn from the same mainstream addiction recovery programs – is that abstinence is historically and statistically an *ineffective* strategy against addiction. Think about it: If we could abstain, we likely wouldn't become addicts in the first place, and we certainly wouldn't be living in the *Great Age of Mediation*.

> **ABSTINENCE IS HISTORICALLY AND STATISTICALLY INEFFECTIVE.**

The indisputable fact, however, is that we can't abstain very well at all, despite any pretense or allusion to the contrary. We can hardly even discuss abstinence without exposing our own rank hypocrisy. Consequently, we are thoroughly immersed and entrenched in our own media consumption habits, morning, noon, and night, not to mention the overwhelming guilt and shame that they often invoke. The media are everywhere we look, and in the very air we breathe. We can simply no longer hope to escape or abstain from the media, and *the jury is in:* Abstinence is simply not a very viable option in the *Great Age of Mediation.*

**ABSTINENCE IS SIMPLY NOT A
VIABLE OPTION IN THE
*GREAT AGE OF MEDIATION.***

That leaves *moderation.* But where do we begin? How do we begin the process of replacing our self-serving rituals with more meaningful rituals? Where do we start? Let's examine the traditional mechanics of addiction recovery. And remember, what begins as a trickle…

The good news is that most addicts recover from their addictions without professional intervention or help. Moreover, almost every successful addiction recovery – with or without professional help – works essentially the same way: We learn how to replace the self-serving rituals and stinking thinking of our addictions with more meaningful rituals, a process that moderates our behavior over time and improves the quality of our lives by definition. Thus, each moment devoted to meaningful ritual is one more moment stolen from the stinking thinking of self-serving ritual.

> **ADDICTION RECOVERY IS THE GRADUAL PROCESS OF REPLACING THE SELF-SERVING RITUALS OF OUR ADDICTIONS WITH MORE MEANINGFUL RITUALS.**

Before we can begin to replace self-serving ritual with more meaningful ritual, however, we must first find a way to disrupt the rhythm of the addiction itself. We must disrupt the addictive cycle. That's why recovery almost always begins with an *intervention* of some sort, sometimes self-imposed, but far more often compelled by one or more outside agents: a spouse, family member, employer, friend, or court order. Intervention is typically portrayed as the overture to the recovery process, but in fact the *entire* recovery process is punctuated by ongoing, persistent intervention while the addict learns to replace the self-serving rituals of addiction with more meaningful ritual over time.

> **ALL ADDICTION RECOVERY BEGINS WITH INTERVENTION, EITHER SELF-IMPOSED OR COMPELLED.**

As recovering addicts, we learn exactly how and when to intervene in the addiction process; we learn how to truncate and modify our own stinking thinking, hopefully before it manifests in more self-serving ritual. Instead of hitting the bar after work, for instance, recovering alcoholics might choose to phone a sponsor or attend an AA meeting instead. The phone calls and the meetings simply represent more meaningful and life-affirming replacement rituals for the self-serving rituals of alcoholism. Likewise, the nicotine addict might choose to take a walk and get some fresh air instead of lighting up another cigarette.

The same mechanics are at work, over and over again, often many times daily, regardless of the narcotic: First we find a way to intervene in and disrupt the addictive cycle, then we effectively replace a self-serving ritual with a more meaningful one.

Intervention and recovery, therefore, are entirely *conscious* acts that require consistently elevated levels of awareness, vigilance, and *gratitude.* By any metric, addiction recovery is a difficult and demanding process imposed on top of what is likely an already difficult and increasingly unmanageable lifestyle – exactly why all addictions are so tough to beat, and why most addicts fail several times before they succeed, if they succeed at all. As with many things in life, however, relentless persistence is the only true predictor of success...

INTERVENTION AND RECOVERY ARE CONSCIOUS ACTS.

The following two chapters will show you how to intervene gently and appropriately in your own life, how to replace your self-serving rituals with more meaningful ritual, and how to improve your life spiritually, physically, emotionally, and socially in the process. They will not show you how to abstain from the media, nor will they show you how to eliminate the media from your life. Rather, they will seek to introduce a measure of sobriety amidst the *Great Age of Mediation*. They will provide the model and tools to help you reintroduce God into your life as a champion and paradigm of *moderation*. In the next two chapters God will become your personal quality control agent, and you will learn exactly how to put Him first – every day...

Chapter 7 Summary

IT'S FAR TOO LATE TO PREVENT
MEDIA ADDICTION IN AMERICA.

WE CAN MAKE THE CHOICE TO IMPROVE
THE QUALITY OF LIFE FOR OURSELVES
AND OUR FAMILIES *TODAY!*

GOD WILL HELP THOSE WHO HAVE
FAITH IN HIM.

ABSTINENCE IS HISTORICALLY AND
STATISTICALLY INEFFECTIVE.

ABSTINENCE IS SIMPLY NOT A
VIABLE OPTION IN THE
GREAT AGE OF MEDIATION.

ADDICTION RECOVERY IS THE GRADUAL
PROCESS OF REPLACING THE
SELF-SERVING RITUALS OF OUR
ADDICTIONS WITH MORE
MEANINGFUL RITUALS.

ALL ADDICTION RECOVERY BEGINS
WITH INTERVENTION, EITHER
SELF-IMPOSED OR COMPELLED.

INTERVENTION AND RECOVERY ARE
CONSCIOUS ACTS.

My Notes

My Notes

Chapter 8
The *Human Centrifuge...*

Dear God,

Teach me to pray. Teach me to listen and to hear. Keep my eyes, ears and heart open to your word. Guide my choices. Help me to turn away from fear and envy and shame, and help me choose behaviors that will draw me closer to you. Help me resist temptation and behave in a manner most pleasing to you and in accordance with your will. Yours and yours alone be done. Amen.

I remember childhood trips with my father to the Fun House at Playland-at-the-Beach in San Francisco some forty-five years ago. I remember the carnival lights, sounds, smells, and flavors like they happened yesterday – still vivid and visceral. I remember the salt air, sharp and sweet, and how little scrap piles of kelp sometimes washed up on shore and glistened in the midday summer sun like an amber necklace along Ocean Beach. I remember the damp and piercing chill of the late afternoon fog as it rolled through, and the distant roar of the Pacific just across the asphalt ribbons of the Great Highway. I remember Laughing Sal, a female mechanical clown whose grotesque visage and cackling laugh presided over the entrance to the Fun House for decades. I remember how my father's eyes widened when he saw her, and how his face brightened, the slumbering child inside him suddenly reawakened and ready to play.

And I remember one Fun House ride in particular: the human centrifuge, a huge wooden turntable that hovered just an inch or two above a worn padded floor. I remember how we all scrambled aboard and plastered ourselves to the great polished disk like animated frescoes, chattering in anxious anticipation. I remember the hum as the motor came alive beneath us and the wheel started to turn, slowly at first, then accelerating, faster and faster until those still clinging to it in extremis suddenly flew off in all directions – screaming in delight. And of course, no one got hurt...

Fade out and fade in, now forty-five years later: Playland-at-the-Beach in San Francisco is gone, long ago demolished and auctioned off, replaced by rows of non-descript seaside condominiums. Some things remain, however: the roar of the Pacific, Ocean Beach, the Great Highway, the fog, the chill, the salt air and, of course, the memories.

Forty-five years later it occurs to me that life in the early 21st-century is very much like the human centrifuge ride of my childhood, very much like the spinning wheel in the Fun House at Playland-at-the-Beach. The adult version, however, runs 24/7, day after day, month after month, year after year. It never stops. It never even slows down. In fact, it accelerates with each revolution. And there's no padding to break your fall if you get tossed off; everyone who gets tossed off gets hurt. Welcome to modern life in the *Great Age of Mediation*.

To properly invoke the human centrifuge as a metaphor for modern life, however, we need to consider three things:

1. *The wheel always spins and never slows down for anyone.* Our job is to withstand the centrifugal force and remain on the wheel at all costs. And if we get tossed off, as sometimes happens, we must climb back on again, irrespective of any injuries or scars we may sustain in the process.

2. *In the absence of countervailing forces or actions, we will always drift by default towards the wheel's outer edge in the Great Age of Mediation.* The centrifugal force generated by the human centrifuge is inexorable, and will *always* act to nudge us outward towards the edge. It therefore doesn't matter which way the wheel turns: clockwise, counterclockwise, liberal, conservative, Demo-

crat, Republican, Christian, Moslem, Jew, Buddhist, or Hindu – the *physics* that govern the wheel are *ordained* from above, constant and inviolate.

3. *Where we are on the spinning wheel at any given point in time will determine the quality of our lives at that moment, and where we spend most of our time on the wheel will determine the general quality of our lives.* In general, life is better towards the center of the wheel (where there is less centrifugal force to battle, and where we are closer to God), and worse towards the outer edge (where the centrifugal force is greatest, and where we are farthest from God). So not only is it important to stay on the wheel, but also to position yourself as close to the center as possible.

THE HUMAN CENTRIFUGE ALWAYS SPINS AND NEVER SLOWS DOWN FOR ANYONE.

ABSENT COUNTERVAILING FORCES OR ACTIONS, WE WILL ALWAYS DRIFT BY DEFAULT TOWARDS LIFE ON THE EDGE IN THE *GREAT AGE OF MEDIATION*.

**THE QUALITY OF OUR LIVES REFLECTS
OUR POSITIONS ON THE
HUMAN CENTRIFUGE.**

The first two conditions above qualify as *force majeure,* pure acts of God, things over which we exert no control whatsoever – no matter how hard we try. Simply stated, the human centrifuge will *always* spin, and will *always* generate centrifugal force, irrespective of our behavior. Only the third condition – where we position ourselves on the wheel – is subject to our own influence.

At any given point in time we will find ourselves positioned on the human centrifuge either closer to God at the center of the wheel, farther removed from God on the wheel's outer edge, or somewhere between the two.

**AT ANY GIVEN TIME, WE WILL FIND
OURSELVES EITHER CLOSER TO GOD IN
THE CENTER OF THE WHEEL, FARTHER
REMOVED FROM GOD AT THE WHEEL'S
OUTER EDGE, OR IN TRANSITION.**

Our addiction to media typically portrays God and religion as the polar opposites and primary threats to reason and enlightenment. According to our addictions, God and religion are invoked only by *extremists* hell-bent on destroying a post-modern world order based on enlightened self-interest, and committed body and soul to casting us back in time to the Middle Ages when theocracies ruled with iron

fists. Nothing, however, could be farther from the truth.
Please note that God is positioned in the *center* of the human
centrifuge for a reason. He's there not because I put Him
there, but because the center of the universe is simply where
He resides. Not at a polar extreme, not as the polar opposite
of evil, and not as the polar opposite of excess. The center of
the universe is God's mailing address. In fact, on the human
centrifuge God represents the *midpoint* between polar extremes. We never have to travel any farther than half way
from anywhere to meet God. He will *always* be there to meet
us at the midpoint.

> **GOD IS IN THE CENTER OF THE HUMAN
> CENTRIFUGE, AT THE MIDPOINT
> BETWEEN POLAR EXTREMES.**

In other words, God represents *moderation in all things,*
the place from whence all things emerge and the place towards which all things once renewed at the end of the day
must *re-converge.* According to the human centrifuge, those
at the polar extremes who invoke God in pursuit of their
own provincial agendas are – in fact – moving farther *away*
from Him, irrespective of any fervent claims to the contrary.
Rest assured that those who would commit murder and
mayhem in God's name will never see His face, and He will
never hear their entreaties. He will only grant an audience
to those who seek *His* justice, not their own. Justice and
vengeance are *His* to dispense, not ours...

**GOD REPRESENTS MODERATION
IN ALL THINGS.**

Let's examine how our position on the wheel affects the quality of our lives, starting from the outer edge then working our way inward. Remember while we do so, however, that our lives are works in progress, and that our position on the wheel can change from day to day, or even from moment to moment, depending on circumstances and the choices we make. That's why we can feel on top of the world at one moment and utterly defeated the next, and why we can exalt in God one minute then find ourselves suddenly wrought with despair the next. God promises to love us and be with us always. But the rest is pretty much up to you and me...

**OUR POSITION ON THE HUMAN
CENTRIFUGE IS SUBJECT TO CHANGE
BECAUSE OUR LIVES ARE ALWAYS IN
TRANSITION.**

**GOD PROMISES TO LOVE US AND BE
WITH US ALWAYS. THE REST IS PRETTY
MUCH UP TO YOU AND ME...**

Life on the Edge...

All of us spend time (perhaps more than we'd like) on the outer edge of the human centrifuge. Indeed, life on the edge is the *default* condition in the *Great Age of Mediation*.

Our paths through life are strewn with the bones and roadside markers of lost loved ones, failed businesses, divorce, unemployment, violence, drugs, alcohol and other addictions, financial problems, and legal hassles. These and other traumatic life events rattle our cages, knock us upside the head, and loosen our grip on the wheel. And sometimes – weary from the day-to-day attrition of the battle just to stay on the wheel – we close our eyes to steal a moment or two of blissful quiet, then wake with a start to find ourselves suddenly drifting right back out towards the edge again. Out there, out where the storm winds blow, we have no time to lick our wounds, and simply brace ourselves for the next big gust. But that's life on the edge in the *Great Age of Mediation*.

Remember, the quality of life is a function of time, of how, where and with whom we spend it. Most of the time we spend on the edge of the wheel is time spent in default *reaction* to the pressures and demands – the centrifugal force – encountered in an *extreme* environment. Little or no time therefore to contemplate right or wrong, little or no time to ponder healthy versus unhealthy or sacred versus profane, and most certainly little or no time for a meaningful relationship with God. Our addiction to media, however, would tell us otherwise: that our utter obsession with all things media is not only benign, but a legitimate and reasonable response to the extreme environments we encounter in life on the edge in the *Great Age of Mediation*.

LIFE ON THE EDGE IS HIGHLY REACTIVE.

Life on the edge keeps us mired in the stressful minutiae and technology-driven exigencies of day-to-day survival. It demands that we spend nearly all of our time just fighting to stay on the wheel, struggling to feed and sustain our obsessions and addictions. But time and energy devoted to the struggle to feed our obsessions and addictions in life on the edge is time and energy diverted *away* from and borrowed against the quality of life. And of course we cannot afford to borrow indefinitely; the quality of life – like all credit lines – is finite.

> **TIME AND ENERGY DEVOTED TO LIFE ON THE EDGE IS TIME AND ENERGY DIVERTED AWAY FROM THE QUALITY OF LIFE.**

The daily skirmishes and battles with our obsessions and addictions carve the harsh landscape, the rollercoaster ups and downs, of life on the edge in the *Great Age of Mediation*. As demonstrated earlier, the immense struggle to maintain and support our fealty and addiction to media consumes almost all of our waking time. Of course no amount of talent, money, or good will can improve our position on the wheel in the absence of time – because we simply cannot buy, beg, borrow, or steal any more of it. And therein resides the real dilemma: In the *Great Age of Mediation*, life on the edge seems full of just about everything except time – and God.

125

> IN THE *GREAT AGE OF MEDIATION*, LIFE
> ON THE EDGE IS FULL OF JUST ABOUT
> EVERYTHING EXCEPT TIME —
> AND GOD.

Ironically, life on the edge is where all of our time is consumed in fealty and addiction to our *time-saving* technologies, especially the media. Ultimately, however, our obsessions and addictions imprison and enslave us. Life on the edge in the *Great Age of Mediation* keeps us thoroughly entertained and thoroughly mesmerized by high-definition and surround-sound technologies, but thoroughly immersed in the glittering gulags of our own obsessions and addictions, and thoroughly removed from a meaningful relationship with God. And unfortunately, life on the edge is precisely where we choose to spend more and more of our time in the *Great Age of Mediation*.

> LIFE ON THE EDGE IMPRISONS AND
> ENSLAVES US, AND KEEPS US
> REMOVED FROM GOD.

Life in Transition...

While we have no choice but to remain on the human centrifuge, and no choice but to endure the ensuing winds, we *are* called upon nevertheless to make the daily choices that – in no small measure – determine our position on the wheel. Free will, after all, is a gift from God – because He wants us to *choose* Him of our own volition. If time is the first gift from God that we sacrifice to our addictions, free will is most certainly the second, because real freedom is represented in the freedom to say no, the freedom to *opt out.* It's the one choice our addictions in the *Great Age of Mediation* don't offer us.

FREE WILL IS A GIFT FROM GOD.

IF TIME IS THE FIRST GIFT FROM GOD THAT WE SACRIFICE TO OUR ADDICTIONS, FREE WILL IS THE SECOND.

REAL FREEDOM IS THE FREEDOM TO OPT OUT.

Functionally, the choices we make – minute by minute, hour by hour, and day by day – either keep us where we are on the wheel, combine with circumstance to move us closer to the outer edge (away from God), or combine with circumstance to move us closer to the center (nearer to God).

THE MANY CHOICES WE MAKE COMBINE WITH CIRCUMSTANCE TO KEEP US MIRED IN OUR OWN INERTIA, MOVE US FARTHER AWAY FROM GOD, OR MOVE US NEARER TO GOD.

127

Our predisposition to choose in ways that promote either the quality of life or our obsessions and addictions depends largely on where we are positioned on the wheel at the time we make our choices. Obsessive-compulsive behavior aside, we are very much creatures of habit, and all behaviors – good, bad, and indifferent – become easier with practice. The closer we are to the outer edge, the more likely we are to predicate our choices on convenience rather than quality, and the more likely we are to slip by default into compulsive behaviors that promote or sustain our obsessions and addictions. Out on the edge we are far more likely to react to our environment, and far more likely to make less considered and ill-informed choices. The longer we live life on the edge, the more difficult it becomes to imagine any other way to live. Protracted exposure to life on the edge inhibits courageous decisions that will help us escape the prison of our addictive behavior and move us closer to God.

THE CHOICES WE MAKE DEPEND LARGELY ON WHERE WE ARE POSITIONED ON THE WHEEL AT THE TIME WE MAKE THEM.

THE CHOICES WE MAKE WHEN WE ARE POSITIONED NEAR THE OUTER EDGE OF THE WHEEL ARE MORE LIKELY TO BE PREDICATED ON CONVENIENCE THAN QUALITY.

Again, it bears repeating that we are almost always in transition on the human centrifuge, almost always moving farther from or closer to God. Our movement in either direction almost always results from a confluence of circumstance and the choices we make from moment to moment, day to day. Movement in either direction is no guarantee that we will be moving in the same direction five minutes from now. The only guarantee is that God wants us to draw nearer to Him. God wants only the best for you and me, guaranteed.

> **THE CHOICES WE MAKE WHEN WE ARE POSITIONED NEAR THE CENTER OF THE WHEEL ARE MORE LIKELY TO BE PREDICATED ON QUALITY THAN CONVENIENCE.**

Life with God...

The closer we are to God, the more likely we are to choose behaviors that *glorify* Him, promote the meaningful relationships *in* our lives, and improve the quality *of* our lives.

Life with God is a fully liberated and wholly *conscious* life. Life surrendered to God is a life of *conscious* decisions predicated on the *deliberate* choice of quality over convenience in an environment less compelled and controlled by our obsessions and addictions. Although life on the edge and life with God are not polar opposites, life with God represents the *antidote* to life on the edge, where the only prerequisite to any decision is pre-programmed fealty to a rigidly erected and enforced status quo. By contrast, life with God offers true freedom of choice.

LIFE WITH GOD REPRESENTS THE ANTIDOTE TO LIFE ON THE EDGE.

You might notice that the above language reverses the common claims made against God and religion by our addiction to media. According to our addictions, a life surrendered to God and religion represents pre-programmed fealty to a rigidly erected and enforced status quo, and a threat to enlightened thinking. But the exact opposite of course is true: In the *Great Age of Mediation*, addiction is the tyrant and God is the liberator. Life with God translates directly into quality time in a quality relationship governed by quality ritual. Life with God invokes His truth to *free* us from the tyranny and false promises of our addictions. Contrary to their self-serving assertions, a life surrendered to God represents the *epitome* of enlightened thinking in the *Great Age of Mediation*.

The table below summarizes the contrasting lifestyle attributes that characterize life on the edge versus life with God…

Life on the Edge	Life with God
▪ Reactive	▪ Proactive
▪ Full of inertia	▪ Liberated
▪ Predicated on quantity	▪ Predicated on quality
▪ More stressful	▪ Less stressful
▪ Hectic and time-starved	▪ Relaxed and composed
▪ Empty and deprived	▪ Full and abundant
▪ Powerless	▪ Powerful
▪ Victim	▪ Victor

Take a moment to review the above table once again, then ask yourself: If the quality of my life is a function of how and where and with whom I spend my time, how and where and with whom would I rather spend it?

The choice you make in response to the above question will help determine your position on the human centrifuge. You can move closer to God and begin to improve the quality of your life right now. It's up to you, but you're not alone. God wants you to succeed, and He will journey with you, step by step...

Chapter 8 Summary

THE HUMAN CENTRIFUGE ALWAYS
SPINS AND NEVER SLOWS DOWN FOR
ANYONE.

ABSENT COUNTERVAILING FORCES OR
ACTIONS, WE WILL ALWAYS DRIFT BY
DEFAULT TOWARDS LIFE ON THE EDGE
IN THE *GREAT AGE OF MEDIATION*.

THE QUALITY OF OUR LIVES REFLECTS
OUR POSITIONS ON THE
HUMAN CENTRIFUGE.

AT ANY GIVEN TIME, WE WILL FIND
OURSELVES EITHER CLOSER TO GOD IN
THE CENTER OF THE WHEEL, FARTHER
REMOVED FROM GOD AT THE WHEEL'S
OUTER EDGE, OR IN TRANSITION.

GOD IS IN THE CENTER OF THE
HUMAN CENTRIFUGE, AT THE
MIDPOINT BETWEEN
POLAR EXTREMES.

GOD REPRESENTS MODERATION
IN ALL THINGS.

OUR POSITION ON THE HUMAN
CENTRIFUGE IS SUBJECT TO CHANGE
BECAUSE OUR LIVES ARE ALWAYS IN
TRANSITION.

Chapter 8 Summary (cont'd)

GOD PROMISES TO LOVE US AND BE
WITH US ALWAYS. THE REST IS PRETTY
MUCH UP TO YOU AND ME...

LIFE ON THE EDGE IS HIGHLY REACTIVE.

TIME AND ENERGY DEVOTED TO LIFE ON
THE EDGE IS TIME AND ENERGY
DIVERTED AWAY FROM THE
QUALITY OF LIFE.

IN THE *GREAT AGE OF MEDIATION*, LIFE
ON THE EDGE IS FULL OF JUST ABOUT
EVERYTHING EXCEPT TIME —
AND GOD.

LIFE ON THE EDGE IMPRISONS AND
ENSLAVES US, AND KEEPS US
REMOVED FROM GOD.

FREE WILL IS A GIFT FROM GOD.

IF TIME IS THE FIRST GIFT FROM GOD
THAT WE SACRIFICE TO OUR
ADDICTIONS, FREE WILL
IS THE SECOND.

REAL FREEDOM IS THE
FREEDOM TO OPT OUT.

Chapter 8 Summary (cont'd)

THE MANY CHOICES WE MAKE COMBINE
WITH CIRCUMSTANCE TO KEEP US
MIRED IN OUR OWN INERTIA, MOVE US
FARTHER AWAY FROM GOD, OR MOVE
US NEARER TO GOD.

THE CHOICES WE MAKE DEPEND
LARGELY ON WHERE WE ARE
POSITIONED ON THE WHEEL AT THE
TIME WE MAKE THEM.

THE CHOICES WE MAKE WHEN WE ARE
POSITIONED NEAR THE OUTER EDGE OF
THE WHEEL ARE MORE LIKELY TO BE
PREDICATED ON
CONVENIENCE THAN QUALITY.

THE CHOICES WE MAKE WHEN WE ARE
POSITIONED NEAR THE CENTER OF THE
WHEEL ARE MORE LIKELY TO BE
PREDICATED ON
QUALITY THAN CONVENIENCE.

LIFE WITH GOD REPRESENTS THE
ANTIDOTE TO LIFE ON THE EDGE.

My Notes

My Notes

Chapter 9
My Ritual Inventory...

Dear God,

Thank you for hearing and answering my prayers. I am so grateful to you for all of the wonderful people and things in my life. Please forgive my many trespasses against you and your word. Help me learn now how to put you first in everything I do. Help me amend my behavior to reflect your will always. Bless this day and show me your favor. Help me live today in adoration and praise of you. Help me avoid those things that steal me away from you, and help me welcome those things that draw me nearer to you. Amen.

An Interview with God.

I dreamed I had an interview with God. "So you would like to interview me?" God asked.

"If you have the time," I said.

God smiled. "My time is eternity...what questions do you have in mind for me?"

"What surprises you most about humankind?"

God answered, "That they get bored with childhood, they rush to grow up, then long to be children again. That they lose their health to make money, then lose their money to restore their health. That by thinking anxiously about the future they forget the present, such that they live in neither the present nor the future. That they live as if they will never die, and die as if though they had never lived.

God's hand took mine and we were silent for a while. And then I asked, "As a parent, what are some of life's lessons you want your children to learn?"

"To learn they cannot make anyone love them. All they can do is let themselves be loved. To learn that it is not good to compare themselves to others. To learn to forgive by practicing forgiveness. To learn that it only takes a few seconds to open profound wounds in those they love, and it can take many years to heal them. To learn that a rich person is not the one who has the most, but is one who needs the least. To learn that there are people who love them dearly, but simply do not know yet how to express or show their feelings. To learn that two people can look at the same thing and see it differently. To learn that it's not enough to forgive one another, but they must also forgive themselves.

"Thank you for your time," I said humbly. "Is there anything else you'd like your children to know?"

"Just know that I am here. Always."

The simple point of this chapter is to offer you a constant reminder that God is here. Always. You can call on him at any time. Every moment is a potential occasion to pray. Remember, we are renewed by the transforming of our minds, one thought at a time...

I suggested way back in Chapter 1 that all quality things share three common traits: Quality is God-given, quality imparts meaning, and quality demands our time and attention. We ascribe value to things when we turn our time and attention to them. I then went on to suggest that our appreciation of quality is an act of commission, and as such likewise demands our time. But appreciation is just another word for *gratitude,* and gratitude is the true foundation of all healing and all quality. If we want quality in our lives, we must set aside time to show our gratitude for it. It's the same with God: If we want Him in our lives, we must first set aside the requisite time to worship and appreciate Him. Faith in God must precede His favor.

GRATITUDE IS THE TRUE FOUNDATION OF ALL HEALING AND ALL QUALITY.

In his wonderful bestselling book about building wealth, *Secrets of the Millionaire Mind: Mastering the Inner Game of Wealth,* author and lecturer T. Harv Eker says:

"Focus on what you have, not on what you don't have. Make a list of ten things you are grateful for in

your life and read the list aloud. Then read it each morn-
ing for the next thirty days. If you don't appreciate what
you've got, you won't get anymore and you don't need
anymore. "

My Ritual Inventory is a simple and proven variation on
the theme mentioned by Mr. Eker above. It's about putting
God first as a daily exercise in gratitude. It's about thanking
Him for all of the wonderful people and things that contribute to the quality of our lives. It's about invoking gratitude
as the driving component of conscious daily intervention,
the first step in the gradual replacement of self-serving ritual
with more meaningful ritual over time. It's about change
that begins as a trickle and becomes a mighty river whose
many tributaries and streams make good our lives and flow
into the City of God. It's about squeezing out our stinking
thinking one thought at a time, about replacing each stinking
thought with one imbued instead with abundance, grace,
and gratitude. It's about invoking God as a *moderating agent*
in the *Great Age of Mediation*, about moving closer to Him
and farther away from life on the edge. *My Ritual Inventory*
will put first things first each time you invoke it. It will right
your thoughts and clear your mind – at least for a little
while. *4 BASIC NEEDS*

There is indeed nothing new under the sun, and every
minute of every day is spent in fealty to and pursuit of one
or more of our four basic needs: spiritual, physical, emotional, and social. The quality of our lives and the quality of the
society we live in is measured in our ability or inability to
satisfy them. God's mystery and glory is revealed through

140

our struggles with them while entire civilizations rise and fall accordingly. Thus has it been for all mankind since the dawn of time, and thus will it remain.

Our exploration of *My Ritual Inventory* therefore begins with a simple definition of meaningful ritual as ***any regularly scheduled activity that enhances and promotes one or more of our four basic needs.***

In practice, the distinctions between self-serving and meaningful rituals are pretty self-evident. For instance, a few quiet minutes spent with a cup of coffee or tea each morning qualifies as meaningful ritual. That same cup of coffee or tea if quaffed in a mad dash out the door does not — even if it happens at the same time every day. Likewise, a morning jog qualifies whereas a frenzied sprint out the door to catch the bus doesn't. Dinner with the family around the dinner table qualifies; stuffing your face with a slice of pizza on the run every evening doesn't. By the same measure, any addiction recovery programs attended on a regular basis qualify, whereas the addictive rituals they address do not. Regularly scheduled biweekly or monthly events — such as book club meetings or theater outings — also qualify. Ad hoc gatherings of family or friends don't. Church every Sunday qualifies, but lifting a prayer to your Higher Power at the race track may not, even if you do it every Sunday right after church. Regular work around the yard or tending the garden qualifies, but breaking out the *Weed Whacker* once every two years doesn't. A cigarette with a snifter of brandy after dinner might constitute a perfectly appropriate evening ritual, as long as the cigarette is not one of forty you inhale

each day, and as long as the brandy doesn't precede or follow a bottle of gin.   NOT DEPENDANT on ELECTRONIC
MEDIA

Table of Meaningful Rituals	
Category	**Meaningful Rituals**
Spiritual	worship and prayer, scripture reading, some music, yoga, meditation, volunteer work, some recovery programs
Physical	exercise, participation sports, yoga, dance, physical therapy, massage, personal grooming, long walks, meditation, cooking, napping, recovery programs
Emotional	therapy, reading, music appreciation, yoga, journal writing, meditation, hobbies, social events with friends, family activities (including meals), recovery programs
Social	family activities (including meals), music appreciation with friends or family, sports and games, work, group therapy, volunteer work, some recovery programs

The above *Table of Meaningful Rituals* is offered as a general guideline, and is by no means complete. You may notice, however, that *none* of the listed rituals – with the sole
exception of music appreciation – rely on or revolve around
electronic media. For the purposes of the following exercise,
those rituals that rely on or revolve around television, the
Internet (including email, instant messaging, social networks, and chat), wireless messaging, and video games *don't*
make the cut for now, even if they enhance and promote one
or more of your four basic needs per the above definition of
meaningful ritual. The *only* exceptions to the rule are those

rituals that revolve around and are specific to making music and/or music appreciation. But don't dismay: *You are perfectly free to indulge in all of your current electronic media consumption habits – with no restrictions whatsoever.* I ask only that you resist the temptation (however strong) to *define* and *list* them as meaningful rituals in the *My Ritual Inventory* exercise that follows.

Let's move on now to the *My Ritual Inventory* worksheet, a working inventory of the meaningful rituals in your life per the above definition.

1. Make and date a copy of the *My Ritual Inventory Worksheet* on the following page.

2. Begin by listing each of the meaningful rituals in your life that you perform on a regularly scheduled basis (for now, don't include any meaningful ritual with a frequency of less than once a month, and don't include your job). List each qualifying ritual only once, regardless of how frequently you repeat it each week or month.

My Ritual Inventory Worksheet					
Meaningful Ritual	Time per mo	SP	PH	EM	SO
Total minutes					
Total hours					

3. After you have listed each of the meaningful rituals that you perform at least once each month, calculate the time you devote each month to each ritual in minutes and write it down in the *Time per month* column. You may need to keep a calculator handy, and it's probably a good idea to use a pencil instead of a pen.

4. After you have calculated the amount of time you devote to each ritual on a monthly basis, assign how the time you spend with each ritual breaks down across each of the four basic needs, represented in the table headings (SP = Spiritual, PH = Physical, EM = Emotional, and SO = Social) per the example table below. (Note: It's perfectly okay for the total amount of time that you assign across all four basic needs to *exceed* the actual time you devote to the ritual.)

My Ritual Inventory Worksheet					
Meaningful Ritual	Time per mo	SP	PH	EM	SO
Prayer walks	120	60	60	60	60
Phone Mike	1200			1200	1200
Exercise	960		960		
Total minutes	2280	60	1020	1260	1260
Total Hours	38	1	17	21	21

145

5. Add *My Ritual Inventory* to the end of your worksheet as a separate meaningful ritual, but don't assign any time figures or basic-need categories.

6. Next, add the total minutes for each column in the *Total Minutes* row, then divide each total by sixty to arrive at the total number of hours devoted to the enhancement of each basic need.

In the above example I listed three meaningful rituals, calculated the monthly time I devote to each in minutes, then assigned specific amounts of time to whichever of the four basic needs each ritual enhanced in my life each month. For instance, I take monthly spiritual walks with a small group from my church and community. We gather one Saturday morning every month, pray and share scripture the first hour, then walk for another hour. The total time spent each month with my group prayer walks is about two hours or 120 minutes. Since the first hour of each get together is strictly prayer and scripture, I entered 60 minutes under SP for spiritual. I also assigned 60 minutes to each of the other three basic needs. Please note that the assignment of time is strictly subjective, and will most certainly change as your life circumstances change. Sometimes we modify the rituals themselves, sometimes we simply grow out of them and set them aside, and sometimes we replace them entirely with others.

As noted above, the total time you assign across all of the categories may and often will exceed the *actual* time you devote to the ritual. For instance, I invest a total of two hours (120 minutes) of actual time each month to my group prayer walks, but I derive four hours (240 minutes) in *perceived* benefits, *twice* the amount I actually invest. That's a pretty good return, and that's *only one* meaningful ritual; it only *hints* at the power of meaningful ritual to change your life for the better, and the inherent wisdom of quality over quantity. My twenty-hour investment of time on the phone with my brother each month returns *forty* hours in perceived emotional and social benefits. Again, a pretty good return by any measure, and even better when we consider that each thought and act dedicated to meaningful ritual is another thought and act stolen away from our supply of stinking thinking and self-serving ritual. The mere fact that our investments in meaningful ritual return so much actual and perceived value is just one of the reasons why I implore you to *take your time* with *My Ritual Inventory,* because you've got an incredibly powerful tool in your hands, and there's more to come...

Using *My Ritual Inventory* as a meaningful ritual

The reason why you added *My Ritual Inventory* to your worksheet is so you can now invoke it daily as a potent meaningful ritual in and of itself. In fact, it was designed specifically to be used as your daily meaningful ritual control center. In it you'll find a convenient and ready source of inspiration whenever and wherever you need one, and a concise guide to all of the people and things that contribute so wondrously to the quality of your life – all on one or two pieces of paper!

In order to invoke *My Ritual Inventory* as meaningful ritual in your life, simply repeat the following two steps for each meaningful ritual on your worksheet:

1. Close your eyes and imagine the ritual for 30-60 seconds. Imagine its unique sights, sounds, aromas, and textures. Imagine how it makes you feel. If it involves other people, imagine their voices, their faces. Meditate for a moment on how it contributes to the enhancement of the assigned basic need(s), and how it improves the quality of your life. In particular, what about it makes you smile and feel loved?

2. Say, "Thank you, God, for blessing and enriching my life with (name the ritual)."

It's that simple. When invoked as a daily ritual, *My Ritual Inventory* becomes a prayer of thanksgiving for all of the good people and things that contribute to the quality of your life. And isn't that what God *wants* us to do? Wouldn't He prefer that we worry less and pray more in the first place?

I like to *begin* each day with *My Ritual Inventory* as a component part of my daily prayer ritual. It imbues me with gratitude and fortifies me for the day ahead. If and when I feel the need for more reinforcement throughout the day or week, I simply take out my worksheet and run through it per the two simple steps above. Each time I do so I rediscover myself, my friends, and my passion for God.

My Ritual Inventory always works, and I can always adjust it to reflect current exigencies and circumstances in my life.

Likewise, you can always perform *My Ritual Inventory* as a tonic for troubled times. It will *always* remind you that you are not alone, that God is with you, and that He wants only good things for you and yours. It will keep you focused on the good people and things in your life; it will keep you focused on God, and forever grateful to Him.

Adding new meaningful rituals to your life

Our lives change. People come and go. Relationships come and go. Sudden and not so sudden changes and disruptions in our lives leave us vulnerable; we find ourselves suddenly back on the outer edge of the human centrifuge, out where we are more likely to choose convenience over quality, out where we are more likely to choose self-serving ritual over meaningful ritual. Consequently, high stress moments, big lifestyle transitions, and moments of sudden change are especially good times to reassess and adjust your ritual inventory. Sudden holes in our lives scream to be filled, and all too often we fill them with self-serving rather than meaningful rituals. *My Ritual Inventory* will help ensure that you don't succumb to convenience over quality when the chips are down, when you most need the presence of quality in your life.

Of course you can invoke *My Ritual Inventory* at any time for any reason, but here's a measured plan to introduce new meaningful rituals over time to help improve the quality of your life, and start moving you closer to God on the human centrifuge. Remember, however, each new meaningful ritual in your life has the potential to generate big returns per the above examples. So let's proceed slowly, and set realistic goals. Let's start with the introduction of just one new meaningful ritual *every other month.* One new meaningful ritual every two months may not sound like a lot of progress, but six new meaningful rituals in your life by the end of the first year can yield *extraordinary* changes.

First, take a few moments to examine the total time you invest in meaningful ritual for each of your four basic needs. Glaring discrepancies in the totals may represent an imbalance in your life wherein some of your basic needs are being satisfied at the possible expense of others. Bear in mind, however, that balance is a relative term, and that how much time you actually invest in meaningful ritual to satisfy each of your four basic needs will doubtless rise and fall as you strive to accommodate changing life circumstances. You may work for months to establish balance in your life across all four basic needs only to experience a sudden seismic event that compels you to reassess and readjust on the fly. For instance, moving to another city to pursue your career may incur long-term benefits across all four basic needs, but the short-term effect will likely be at least physically, emotionally, and socially disruptive – and will likely remain so until you re-establish new relationships and meaningful rituals in your new hometown to restore the balance.

Next, identify your weakest basic need, defined as the basic need with the lowest *perceived* time value on your *My Ritual Inventory* worksheet. Over the next week, make it your assignment to identify and incorporate one new meaningful ritual that will enhance and promote your weakest basic need. Finally, add your new meaningful ritual to your

My Ritual Inventory worksheet and adjust the time totals accordingly; your new meaningful ritual will now assume its place as part of your daily *My Ritual Inventory* review.

Although *My Ritual Inventory* is an incredibly powerful and effective lifestyle improvement tool, it simply cannot help you manufacture more time. So if you're wondering exactly how or where you'll find the time to incorporate another meaningful ritual into your already busy schedule, you need look no further than the *Media Log* worksheet that you created back in Chapter 4. That's where you'll doubtless find the time you need to introduce new meaningful rituals into your life. Remember, it's not about finding more time; it's about replacing self-serving ritual with more meaningful ritual.

Repeat the above process once every other month: Identify your weakest basic need, take a week to find and introduce a new meaningful ritual, add it to your worksheet, and adjust the time totals.

In general, you should look for meaningful rituals that promote moderation over abstinence. And don't overreach; don't set yourself up for failure by expecting yourself to perform miracles, even and especially if you are a classic overachiever. Make modest investments, seek modest gains and let the principle of compounding interest work for you, not only with your money but with your life as well. One year from now you'll enjoy six more meaningful rituals in your life, each contributing disproportionately and aggressively to the overall quality of your life. Moreover, the desire and need to examine and adjust the meaningful rituals in our lives on an ongoing basis is entirely consistent with the fact that the centrifugal force generated by the human centrifuge pushes us inexorably towards life on the edge and *away* from God. *My Ritual Inventory* will help nudge you over time *back* from the outer edge and closer and closer towards the center, nearer and nearer to God. Remember, the quality of your life demands *your* active participation. Do your part with faith in Him, and He will do His.

We can't stop the human centrifuge from spinning, and we certainly can't stop the centrifugal force winds from blowing. But we can choose God over life on the edge each and every day. We can choose to put God first, not merely as an alternative to life on the edge, but as a fully integrated, perfectly attuned lifestyle strategy for the *Great Age of Mediation*. Meanwhile, rejoice in the Lord! Rejoice and give thanks. May He look down in favor and grace upon you. May you walk in His light always...

About Jeff Einstein

Who better to write about the confluence of media, addiction, and God than a Born Again ex-addict who also happens to be a nationally recognized digital media pioneer?

Mr. Einstein's digital media chops date back to 1984 when he co-founded EASI, the nation's first digital advertising agency. Since then his media work has been featured in virtually every major business print venue, including two front-page articles in *The Wall Street Journal,* and cover stories for *George, Red Herring Magazine, PC Magazine,* and *The New York Times Sunday Magazine.* He has appeared as a media industry expert in dozens of TV and radio interviews, including *CNN 360* with Anderson Cooper and *The Today Show* with Katie Couric.

He's also a published author with nine titles to his credit, and a syndicated columnist. His controversial writings on media and addiction have been published and re-published on literally thousands of websites and weblogs, and he's appeared nationwide as a featured speaker and lecturer at hundreds of trade shows, seminars, and workshops over the past two decades.

Mr. Einstein lives in a quiet suburb of NYC, and serves on the Board of Christian Education for a local Congregational church. His greatest achievement, however, is "…a beautiful little girl who never fails to make my heart sing…"

SEE THIS MATTER OF FEAR   PP65

(LANGUAGE OF THE HEART)

Printed in Great Britain
by Amazon

40529515R00108